Transforming Leadership

Transforming Leadership

A Christian Approach to Management

RICHARD HIGGINSON

First Published 1996
SPCK
Holy Trinity Church
Marylebone Road
London
NW1 4DU

NOTE
Unless otherwise indicated, biblical quotations are from
the *Revised Standard Version of the Bible* © 1971 and 1952.
The *New International Version* (NIV) is © 1973,
1978, 1984 by the International Bible Society. Published
by Hodder & Stoughton.
The *Good News Bible* (GNB) is published by The Bible
Societies/HarperCollins Publishers Ltd UK © American
Bible Society, 1966, 1971, 1976, 1992.

British Library Cataloguing-in-Publication Data

A catalogue record for this book is available from the
British Library.

ISBN 0-281-04830-4

Typeset by Pioneer Associates, Perthshire
Printed in Great Britain by
The Cromwell Press, Melksham, Wiltshire

Contents

Preface

This book is based on the 1994 London Lectures in Contemporary Christianity. It was a great honour to be invited to give these lectures and I should like to thank Rev. Dr Ernest Lucas, then Education Director at Christian Impact, and the other members of the organizing committee, for asking me to fulfil this exacting but exciting role.

I was also delighted to have as chairpersons for the different lectures four leaders whose friendship, support and stimulus have meant a great deal to me over recent years: Lady Judith Wilcox, Chairman of the National Consumer Council; James Allcock, formerly Director of Gas Supplies at British Gas, and now consultant to the energy industry; Patrick O'Ferrall, Chairman of Lloyd's Register of Shipping; and Andrew Phillips, Senior Partner at Bates, Wells and Braithwaite, solicitors.

Thank you too for the people who attended those lectures. I was impressed by the consistency of turn-out; many people attended all four. The questions which were asked at the end of the lectures have been a spur to me in further developing and refining my thinking. I have therefore incorporated into this book reflections on some of those questions. I have also added a first chapter, which lays foundations for the other four by outlining a theology of work, and a postscript on the character of Daniel.

The theme of *Transforming Leadership* is one that neatly sums up most of the major topics we have sought to cover in seminars run under the Ridley Hall Foundation programme since 1989. I have organized four- and two-day seminars on Issues of Leadership, Values in Business,

Managing Change, and Success and Failure in Business. What follows is an encapsulation of some of the key insights which have emerged during the course of those seminars. As such, they draw liberally on the experience and views of many who attended the seminars, and I am grateful to them as well. When it comes to speaking and writing I am an unashamed parasite: always ready to use other people's bright ideas! I just hope that most of the time I manage to pay due acknowledgement.

In choosing the title *Transforming Leadership*, I have given in to a besetting temptation to choose titles which can be taken more than one way. Just as *Faith in Business* (the sub-title of the Ridley Hall Foundation) and *Called to Account* (an earlier book on Christianity and business) are riddled with double or even triple entendres, so it is the case with this title. 'Transforming' can be taken either as an adjective or a verb. I want to consider the type and style of leadership which is transforming – which has a transforming effect on organizations and situations. I also want to consider how leadership can be transformed – and how we, as leaders or potential leaders, can be transformed. And I shall be doing so, as faithfully and authentically as I can, from a Christian perspective.

Despite the recent publication of more than one Christian book proclaiming that 'leadership is male', I have not made that assumption in this book. I have varied my use of the personal pronoun, sometimes referring to leaders as 'he' and sometimes as 'she'. The questions of whether God intended leadership to be exercised by one gender rather than the other, or whether men and women tend to exercise leadership in different ways, are interesting ones, but they fall outside the scope of this book.

As I have delved further into the area of leadership, I have realized just how big an area it is. This book makes no claim to be a comprehensive coverage of the subject. I am simply focusing on certain aspects which I find to be of particular interest. So without further ado, let's begin.

1

Hidden Treasure

Redeeming the World of Work

Most Christian books on leadership are about leadership in the local church. They are concerned with the leading of congregations, house groups or youth work. To a contemporary church crying out for encouragement, revival and reform, they seek to apply new insights from the Bible, modern business literature, or a combination of the two.

An example of the type of book I mean is John Finney's *Understanding Leadership*.[1] The blurb on the back cover provides a reliable indication of what the book is about:

> What is the basis of good leadership? How should change be dealt with? How can church members be encouraged to fulfil their potential? These are some of the crucial questions which John Finney addresses in this immensely practical book.
>
> In assessing leadership, he stresses the importance of scripture and of following biblical patterns of authority. But the Church is also a very human organisation and the book shows how management techniques can be used to teach us more about how people relate to each other, how they can be encouraged to work together, and how they can achieve their goals.

I need to emphasize that I believe there is a very proper place for such books, and Finney's is an excellent example of this type. But I have not sought to add to their number here. This is because I am convinced that there is a contrasting shortage of literature written for Christians seeking

to exercise their responsibility as leaders in the wider
world. Similarly, there is little in the programme of most
local churches which addresses the problems of integrating
different personality types in the workplace; of maintaining
high standards of professional integrity while loyally pursuing corporate goals; of nursing an organization through
a traumatic process of change; or of responding constructively to the inevitable episodes of failure which punctuate
experience at work. Yet these are the sort of issues which
preoccupy the minds and emotions of many church members, from Monday to Friday and frequently on Saturday.
Reform, restructuring and revival (in short, transformation)
is needed at work, as well as in the organization of the
church.

Transforming Leadership is concerned with the practical
outworking of Christian discipleship in an increasingly secular world. What does it mean to be a leader in the world
of politics, business, public service or charitable organizations? Do the same Christian principles of leadership
apply, or is it necessary to abandon or radically dilute them?
Does the Christian have distinctive insights or resources on
which he or she can draw? These are the type of questions
considered here.

A little more needs to be said about the areas of life I
am seeking to cover in addressing this subject of leadership.
Because of the specific focus of the work of the Ridley
Hall Foundation, it is the sphere of business which comes
particularly under the microscope. I understand the word
'business' very broadly: it includes both the manufacturing and service sectors, and it also embraces professions
which may seem to be on the periphery of business, such
as accountancy and law. Business provides a searching
test-case for exploring the relevance of faith to public life,
because there is frequently felt to be considerable tension
between business values and Christian values, and the
church often has difficulty in reacting to business with

anything other than hostility or suspicion. It is precisely the size of this challenge which has lent fascination to my involvement with the business community over the last few years. Middle as well as senior managers should find much in these pages which strikes chords with their experience.

However, the relevance of this book will not be limited to the area of business. I am convinced that the fundamental principles of good leadership apply across the board, to a wide range of occupational sectors and types of organization. As well as directing the Ridley Hall Foundation and being a member of the Ridley Hall Theological College Tutorial staff, I am a governor at a local primary school and father to a family of five children. The themes of leadership are relevant to all these areas of my life. They occupy the mind frequently! Even those who head quite small organizations or take initiatives in the local community can benefit much by reflecting on the nature of good leadership.

Transforming Leadership also engages at various points with some of the more significant business literature on leadership. There is no shortage in the western world today of people handing out advice: just as management consultants abound, so do business gurus. Some of this writing is without doubt ephemeral and gimmicky. I have very little time for the 'how to . . .' type of book such as *How to Develop a Perfect Memory*, *How to Manipulate Meetings* or *How to Make a Killing in the Share Jungle*. While these books sometimes contain sound business advice, they are quite unreflective in making single-minded pursuit of personal interests the sole matter of concern. They exalt technique at the expense of respect for other people.

Almost all business literature, in fact, contains implicit or explicit advice on how the reader might improve his or her performance. In its more sophisticated form, however, it contains penetrating analysis of current trends, and prophetic identification of new ones – often presented in a popular guise to assist in spreading the message. I have in mind writers like John Adair, Charles Handy, Tom Peters and Peter Drucker. The size of fee they are able to command for the pleasure of hearing them speak bears testimony to the respect with which they are held in the business community. Such people represent a genre of modern writing with which the Christian community ought to be interacting rather more than is currently the case.

Why Bother?

The question may well be asked, however, why Christians should be so concerned with the world of work in the first place. Some Christians – surprisingly, even some in quite senior positions – tend to regard work as a necessary evil. They see work as a means of making ends meet, so that one is then able to pursue and finance the really interesting things which go on outside working hours. Much of their time may be spent at work, but most of their creative energy goes elsewhere, often into activities at church. Where that is the case, transforming leadership in the workplace does not feature seriously on the agenda. It could be a serious diversion from what Christians should really be about: evangelizing their neighbour and keeping themselves 'unspotted from the world', a duty which often gets restricted in workplace terms to not swearing and not stealing the paper-clips!

This book is based on a much more positive understanding of the relationship between faith and work. It sees daily work as a sphere for which God gifts people and to which God calls people. The talents with which God has equipped men and women include a fine eye for financial detail, skill in resolving conflict, and dexterity with one's hands. Talents like these can go a long way to making the world, not just the church, a significantly better place. Using the language of Martin Luther, the 'stations' in which we find ourselves (for example, engineer, secretary and social worker, as well as parent, spouse and councillor) can all constitute genuine vocations in which we are called to serve God and love our neighbour.[2]

Likewise, a positive understanding of work sees the summons of Jesus to be 'the salt of the earth' and 'the light of the world' as taking expression, first and foremost, in the place where people spend most of their time. Salt preserves and light warns: we have a responsibility to resist evil influences and alert to moral danger in the workplace. Salt flavours and light guides: we have a responsibility to enhance what is good and witness to Christ. Above all, salt glistens and light shines: we have a responsibility to be true to our nature, authentically, visibly Christian. Jesus does not give us the option of choosing when and where to be salt and light. If salt becomes contaminated, so that it loses its saltiness, or light is perversely hidden, the verdict Jesus gives is unmistakable: it is good for nothing! (Matthew 5.13-16).

A similarly positive approach to work is implicit in Paul's words in Romans 12.1-2. Paul exhorts his readers to 'present your bodies as a living sacrifice, holy and acceptable to God, which is your spiritual worship.' The vision is holistic: everything Christians do should be fit for offering to God in his service.

Paul continues: 'Do not be conformed to this world but be transformed by the renewal of your mind . . .' Notice the radical language of *transformation*. Christians in the workplace should not unthinkingly go along with the world's way of doing things. As people whose minds have been and are being renewed, they are concerned to 'prove what is the will of God, what is good and acceptable and perfect'. 'Prove' in this context has the meaning of 'discern', i.e. identify through a process of weighing and testing. A renewed mind chews over issues carefully and prayerfully. It does not automatically reject fashionable opinion, nor does it follow it slavishly. It is no longer 'conformed', because fresh influences and fresh perspectives have been brought to bear upon the issues under consideration. The New Testament presents the Holy Spirit as the great source of personal renewal.

In my book *Called to Account*, I presented a systematic overview of the world of business from a Christian perspective. Each chapter illuminated detailed business scenarios by the light of a different Christian doctrine (for example, God as Trinity). My conviction is that from the first statement of the creed to the last, Christian faith is relevant – excitingly, if sometimes unexpectedly, relevant. I shall not attempt anything so comprehensive here, but simply present work under the spotlight of four key stages in the Christian drama of salvation: creation, fall, redemption, and our future hope.

Creation-with-fall

The first key stage is that of *creation*. God has created the world and all that is in it – and as the climax of his creation he has made human beings, who are themselves creative and called to be responsible managers of his creation. It is important not to make the kindergarten theological error of thinking that work comes in only after the fall. On the contrary, work was part of God's original design for humanity. It is good and necessary for people to work: necessary, for our survival, and good, because it fulfils certain needs and aspirations which God has put within us. Work is one of the key areas where we have scope for applying our rationality, exercising moral choice, interacting in relationships, and discovering our creativity. All of these contribute to what it means to be made 'in the image of God' (Genesis 1.26).

Genesis 1 and 2 provide two contrasting but complementary pictures of our relationship with the world in
which God has placed us. In one, men and women are
told to 'subdue' the earth and 'have dominion' over living
creatures. It hints of a major struggle with the elements,
which humans are given permission to master. In the
other, Adam is put in the garden to 'till it and keep it'.
Here the relationship is more that of friendly companion.

A similar balance is found if we take together two well-
known phrases from the Psalms. Psalm 8 says that God
has made man ruler of creation: 'You made him ruler over
the works of your hands; you put everything under his feet:
all flocks and herds and the beasts of the field . . .' (Psalm
8:6-7, NIV). But it is a rule which needs to be exercised
humbly, carefully and compassionately, and with the
awareness of being accountable to God, for 'the earth is
the Lord's, and everything in it' (Psalm 24.1, NIV). Our
position is that of stewards, not absolute rulers. The earth
is God's gracious provision to us as a dwelling-place, and
should be treated with respect.

Nevertheless – and this is where business comes in –
there is a major task to be performed by men and women
in terms of the wise use of the world's resources. God has
so constructed the world that most of its resources require
some process of extraction, conversion and refinement
before they can be of benefit. This is true both of resources
which lie above the earth's surface (cotton to make shirts,
sugar to make sweets) and those which lie below (coal and
gas to provide warmth and energy). Here lies the essence
of manufacturing industry: *adding value to original resource*.
The more sophisticated the industry, of course, the more
processed is the nature of the primary material, such as the
micro-chip in the construction of computers. Many of the
heavy manufacturing industries have passed their heyday,
and we have now moved towards a greater emphasis on
ancillary services, such as financial services which provide

the venture capital and help to manage the element of risk. But it is mistaken to think that we will ever change to a wholly service economy. As long as human beings survive on planet earth, they will be endeavouring to develop material resources in ever more efficient and ingenious ways.

There is a very proper theology of *wealth creation*, then, which corresponds to the task we have of adding value to God-given resources in creation. This way of understanding it is crucial. Wealth creation is partly about making money; a company that markets a product successfully will do that. Through corporate taxation, some of this money passes through the hands of the exchequer to finance public services and create working opportunities for many others in the community. But wealth creation is also about providing direct benefits to the community and adding to the quality of people's lives; a company that turns out a really useful product will do that also. Companies which make trash products or seriously damage the environment are not creating wealth in any meaningful sense. They are destroying value more than they are adding it.

This darker side of corporate activity brings us to the second key aspect of Christian understanding – *the fall*. I use this term as a piece of theological shorthand, not because I am committed to a literalistic interpretation of the Genesis story of Adam and Eve taking the forbidden fruit. It is simply a way of expressing the fact that human beings have fallen from their high calling, and that they deviate from God's purposes for them and his world in a great variety of ways.

The world of work, just like other spheres of life, shows human sinfulness in abundance: the fact that increased profit can become an idol which subverts all else; the ruthless asset-strippers who become blind to the human cost in their buying and selling of companies; the attitude of endemic dishonesty which can become rife in certain corporate cultures; the manager who deliberately buries himself behind a desk or a secretary to cut himself off from the pain being suffered by others; the fact that people develop radically schizophrenic attitudes about work and the rest of life, countenancing actions in one which they wouldn't dream of in the other. Christians can easily find themselves caught up in this fallen spiral along with everybody else.

It is also worth reflecting on the number of jobs which are an explicit response to the sinful dimension of humanity. Some essentially collaborate with it, like pimps and prostitutes who make a living out of the fact that many men's sexual lives are disordered; or people in the tobacco industry, exploiting a different kind of addiction. Others seek to counteract it: doctors and nurses, coping with the ravages of avoidable illnesses and accidents; policemen seeking to prevent and detect crime; social workers trying to restore harmony in families; locksmiths, and elements of the insurance industry, earning a living through the fact that we cannot trust others not to steal our property. A world without sin would have much to commend it, but it would put a sizeable part of society out of a job!

But the fall is not only reflected in human deviousness, deliberate perversity or attempts to wage war against such things. The fall is also evident in the imbalances and distortions which can be seen in the world of work, in what is sometimes called structural sin, where it is much harder to pinpoint individual blame. It is a mark of the world's fallenness that societies struggle to get a good balance between the number of people able and willing to work, and the number of jobs available; or the fact that most people seem to be either over-worked or under-worked, with few enjoying that happy balance between the two. It is a black mark on our society, not just on particular organizations, that this is the case. Here again, the Bible depicts the fall as affecting work in its very essence. In place of the idyllic conditions of the Garden of Eden, Genesis 3 speaks of sweat and toil, thorns and thistles. Despite the advances made by modern technology, it seems impossible to exclude from many types of job some element of hard, grinding work, and tedious, monotonous routine.

For many Christians, relating theological categories to the world does not get beyond the two just cited. If they find themselves in an unsatisfying job, or they are conscious of low moral standards in their sector of work, it is the doctrine of the fall which is uppermost in their minds. If they are fortunate enough to have a job which they find stimulating, where they are able to develop their gifts, it is more likely to be the doctrine of creation. What most of us experience, most of the time, is a mixture of the two: creation-with-fall; God's gracious provision of work, grievously flawed. But even taken together, these Old Testament categories are not enough. An authentically Christian understanding of work needs to contain the dimensions of redemption and future hope. For many people, accommodating these is more problematic.

New Beginnings

Christians down the ages have unpacked the nature of Jesus' saving work in terms of a doctrine of *redemption*. A redeemer is one who brings about the freedom of others by delivering a payment. Jesus buys back the freedom of the human race by paying for their sin in his death. He gives sacrificially of himself, on others' behalf. This is a great deal more relevant to the world of work than might be obvious at first sight.

First, the redeemer is somebody who is content to play a servant role. The focus of his actions is the well-being of others. This dimension is implicitly present in all types of work. It may appear to be most obvious in the case of the 'caring professions', but it is also a familiar concept in the commercial world: the phrase 'serving the customer' is one which passes a businessperson's lips often enough. But they are empty words if the customer becomes an object of scorn, manipulation or indifference, which can happen all too easily. Christians in business, as in other spheres, should have a solid commitment to a genuine ideal of service.

When we stop to think about goods and services which we easily take for granted, we see that a variety of people have often worked extremely hard and gone to great lengths to provide them. In his book *Working with God*, Andrew Stokes gives the example of the prepared salad or oven-ready meal you take off the supermarket shelf: 'You will only find them if someone else left their children and fireside yesterday evening and stood at a processing line washing or packing, if another person left a warm bed and drove through the small hours to deliver them, and another checked them into the chill room at the back.'[3] Doing a job well often means going the extra mile, making that little additional effort.

Second, taking the life and ministry of Christ seriously sets before us the possibilities of a *new start*. Redemption signifies deliverance from the power of evil, passing from darkness into light, making a new beginning – all the metaphors used in the New Testament about the salvation God has wrought in Christ have a stark, dramatic character. In 2 Corinthians 3.18, Paul says that 'we all, with unveiled face, beholding the glory of the Lord, are being changed into his likeness from one degree of glory to another.' This is no minor transformation!

The consequence of taking such statements seriously is that we should not be fatalists, giving up humanity and human structures as a lost cause. Life on earth will always partake of the character of the fall, involving struggle, disappointments and reversals. Paul in the very next chapter of 2 Corinthians, chapter 4, emphasizes that. But the fact of Christ's coming gives us hope: hope that there is a force for good in the world, hope that some at least of the unsatisfactory aspects of the workplace can be changed.

One unsatisfactory aspect is that much of our work since the Industrial Revolution has been organized in such a way that it has a deformed character. Individuals have too often been treated as mere functionaries, deprived of the opportunity to apply creative and critical thought to their work, or trapped in the tedium of repetitively performing a single function on the assembly line. But work does not have to be organized like that. Through his interesting book, *To Live and Work*,[4] and his consultancy, Work Restructuring, Christian Schumacher has argued that for work to be satisfying, it needs to partake of the three elements of planning, doing and reviewing. Everyone should have the opportunity to apply creative and critical thought to the work with which they are involved. He therefore advocates the organization of companies into small work-groups, so that all may experience the satisfaction of 'whole work'.[5] Over the last decade this type of restructuring has taken place in many organizations, not least the car industry, where Volvo's small group experiment, in which individuals perform a variety of tasks within a recognized group responsibility, set a lead which other manufacturers have gradually followed.

Schumacher also believes that job satisfaction is linked to the extent to which work is related to an organization's core activity. This core activity consists, typically, in a process of *transformation*, whereby raw materials are changed into something both different and valuable, whether it be the baking of bread, the forging of steel, or even the healing of a patient. There is often scope for streamlining an organization so that every individual and group partakes less of tedious, trivial activities, and is more involved in the fundamental process which gives meaning and purpose to the whole enterprise. True, there will always be certain ancillary operations, peripheral to the basic process of transformation, but there is an increasing trend to sub-contract these to other organizations, who make them into their core activity.

Lack of satisfaction for employees is one form of blight in the workplace; lack of satisfaction for customers is another, and this is even more serious. Where the ideal of service is poorly developed or tarnished through neglect, something needs to be done about it – quickly. So a senior manager may have a crucial role to play in sweeping the evil, represented by complacency with low standards and indifference to customer needs, out of the system. In critical situations he may need to take very radical steps: removing people, reforming practices and replacing products. Effectively, he is making a new start.

It may well be asked what is redemptive about such a course of action. Surely this calls to mind not the image of Jesus on the cross, but Jesus expelling the money-changers from the temple (though that incident in itself may suggest that there is a valid place for such action)? Surely it conforms to the conventional, macho image of management? Radical action may indeed be carried out in precisely that mould – but not necessarily. There may well be considerable cost involved for the wielder of the new broom. The action he takes will almost certainly be to the client's or customer's benefit, but it is still likely to provoke considerable resistance from within the organization. People do not like being stirred out of their cosy little ruts. Just as Jesus did when he evacuated the temple, the senior manager will experience resentment and pick up flak.

This brings us to a third key consideration, which is that radical transformation of a situation is rarely possible without cost. Individuals and groups have to be willing for change, including self-sacrificial change, if work is to be conducted in the way it should be – the way that God desires. Actions which have a transforming effect often have the character of costly Christ-likeness.

So there may be times when Christians at work are called to take a costly decision or make a costly protest. The issue at stake may be one of the lengths (or depths) to which they are prepared to go to win an important contract. It may be the morally dubious nature of the company or customer with which they are being asked to do business. It may be a trend towards taking short cuts in matters affecting employee and public safety.

The person who speaks up about such issues will probably not be very popular. There is often resistance to those who work for moral improvement. In the end, the person could be marginalized, ostracized, or even forced to resign. On the other hand, Christians at work are sometimes pleasantly surprised to discover that when they stand up for their convictions, others actually respect them for it. Colleagues may even be grateful for someone who is willing to take a moral lead and to act as a corporate conscience – and they might then be prepared to follow. But there is no guarantee of this. Taking a moral stand is risky, and the Christian may end up like Jesus, going it alone.

Another type of self-sacrifice is when we realize that we have outlived our usefulness in a particular sphere of work. The situation now calls for someone with rather different skills; it is time that we moved on. A company which initially required the dynamic and innovatory gifts of the entrepreneur may in time require a less flamboyant period of consolidation, calling for a different style of leadership. But how hard it usually is for the founder-owner to let go! Nevertheless, I can honestly report that over the last year I have met three different people who have knowingly consented to a process of restructuring, for the corporate good, which involved the loss of their own job.

Most of these examples of sacrificial activity in the workplace involve individuals. It is more difficult to see the relevance of redemption for corporate institutions, which are expected, almost as part of their very definition, to fight for their survival. But corporate groups which believe in survival at all costs often sow the seeds of their own destruction. In a bitter industrial dispute, progress can often only be made when one side – preferably the more powerful side – takes the initiative in conceding something. In a highly competitive market, selling your company to another, which is better equipped for long-term growth and prosperity, may be the far-sighted thing to do. In the world of charitable organizations, merging one body with another, whose aims are compatible or overlapping, could be a way of channelling donations and using resources more effectively.

No organization has a divine right to success, or to ever-lasting life. If it no longer has the capacity to perform a useful role, then its continued existence may rightly be questioned. Most of the time, however, asking that question will be an unhelpful diversion from the whole-hearted endeavour and quality of service which will help to guarantee that the organization does have a continuing role.

The dimension of hope

The final stage in the biblical drama of salvation is one that is still to come. It is the *hope of a future world*, where everything is in perfect harmony. The opening verses of Revelation 21 describe this in terms of 'a new heaven and a new earth', 'a holy city, the new Jerusalem, coming down out of heaven from God, prepared as a bride adorned for her husband'. This future world is also a place where there is no longer any need for a temple, for a demarcation between the sacred and the secular, because 'its temple is the Lord God the Almighty and the Lamb' (verse 22).

The phrase 'a new heaven and a new earth' also occurs in Isaiah 65.17-25. Here the prophet's expectation of a Golden Age lies squarely within the confines of earthly history. He sees Jerusalem as the focus of this transformed existence. He is still thinking in terms of human mortality, even though everyone is now guaranteed of living to a good old age. 'No more shall there be . . . an infant that lives but a few days,' he says, 'or an old man who does not fill out his days' (verse 20). But the extent of the transformation is so great, the vision of life so Utopian, that it is hard from our perspective to believe that this will ever be realized within history. Will there ever be an end to all conflict in the animal kingdom ('the wolf and the lamb shall feed together' – verse 25)? Can we truly imagine no more annexation of people's property ('they shall not build and another inhabit' – verse 22)? We are certainly no closer to such idealized conditions than the Jews were at the time of the prophet's writing.

The fact is that we live in an age when snakes still bite, young people are tragically cut short in their prime and the little guy easily gets trampled on by the corporation with industrial muscle. Hope is often at odds with current experience. For a whole variety of reasons, we may have to settle for something that is less than ideal. There is an honourable Christian place for compromise, about which I will say more in chapter three.

Yet it is very important not to lose the dimension of hope. The hope which we have as Christians for a better world ought to excite us. We should embrace it with so eager a desire, that we do in fact allow it to transform – even revolutionize – our present. Although we may not realize it, this is essentially what we are asking every time we pray the Lord's Prayer. It is intrinsically connected to the nature of Jesus' teaching about the kingdom of God.

What, after all, does it mean to request that God's kingdom will come? The very next phrase supplies the answer: that God's will should be done on earth, as perfectly as it already is in heaven. It was also perfectly carried out by Jesus himself during his time on earth. The kingdom has dawned in Jesus, but it is incomplete, and it will only arrive in its entirety with his second coming. Nevertheless, the ministry of Jesus in word and deed – the example of complete dedication to his Father's will which his life provides – has given us a picture of what that kingdom is like. Our own lives are to be transformed in the light of Jesus' embodiment of kingdom values.

If we are sincere in making the request that God's kingdom should come, then we open ourselves up to the possibility that it will indeed be granted, that we may actually be agents of doing God's will. By simple acts of obedient discipleship, we play a part in bringing the present world into closer conformity with that glorious future age of which the biblical passages speak. Situations, not just individuals, can be changed for the better.

In the world of work we may only get occasional glimpses of this, but there are moments worth savouring. Just as there are episodes of awful tedium and depressing futility at work, so there can also be moments of exciting transformation. Examples might include the glow of satisfaction over a finished product, one which has taken a lot of money, time and effort to achieve, but which produces a sense of exhilaration because of the benefits it will bring to those who buy it; the unravelling of manipulative accounting practice, so that confusion and corruption are brushed away and the true state of financial affairs is clearly revealed: or the breakdown of hierarchical structures which have impeded progress, and the establishment of confidence and goodwill between those once dubbed blue and white collar workers.

All these and other things are well worth striving for. As another writer on the theology of work has written: 'Through the Spirit, God is already working in history, using human actions to create provisional states of affairs that anticipate the new creation in a real way.'[6] It is right to be excited when substantial progress is made in the direction of any one of them. What is created on earth may

seem to be something which is only of temporal signifi-
cance, but it could be that God has some surprises in store
for us.

There is an intriguing reference in Revelation 21.24–26
to the kings of the earth bringing into the heavenly city
'the glory and honour of the nations'. In his commentary
on Revelation, Michael Wilcock takes this to mean that
'all that is truly good and beautiful will reappear there,
purified and enhanced in the perfect setting its Master
intended for it; nothing of real value is lost'.[7] One would
like to think that this includes some at least of what is done
in the world of work.

The preceding pages have allowed scope only to sketch
a theology of work. Much more could be said. The work of
redemption, for instance, could be broken down into the
distinct episodes of Jesus' incarnation, crucifixion and resurrection, and analogies could be drawn between these
events and the processes which take place at work. But the
overall theological framework should be clear. I believe it
provides a series of motifs for making sense of the world
in which people live and work. This is the context in
which some people are called to exercise leadership. The
assumption in the chapters which follows is that transformation is as fundamental to understanding the role of
leadership as it is to appreciating the Christian's calling in
the world more generally.

Hidden Treasure

One image which Jesus used of the kingdom of heaven
was that of *hidden treasure*. 'The kingdom of heaven is like
treasure hidden in a field, which a man found and covered
up; then in his joy he goes and sells all that he has and
buys that field' (Matthew 13.44). A vibrant, relevant
theology of work has something of the character of hidden
treasure. It may not have an overt impact on most of the

work people do most of the time. But it is well worth unearthing periodically in order to reassess one's goals, values and methods in the arena of work. It provides distinctive insights which will sometimes lead Christians down roads unpursued by other people. It sets work within the overall purposes of God, and no Christian should be so absorbed with the here-and-now that he or she loses that wider perspective.

The Christian faith is actually a crucial piece of management data. It provides essential clues for understanding who people are, why things go wrong, and how situations can be changed for the better. If that seems a bold claim, it chimes in with an observation which I hear increasingly often, that the best in modern management theory is really Christianity in secular guise. There is a lot of truth in this. I recall a meeting where a Professor of Business Studies told a group of clergy that the organizational world is 'stealing your clothes'. In the remainder of the book I shall draw attention to a number of resonances between secular and Christian thinking. Sometimes the correspondence may be due to the fact that business gurus are Christians, though not writing explicitly as such. But often it is simply the fact that Christian concepts like forgiveness, servant leadership and peace of mind are key constituents in functioning effectively, and those who are shrewdest in their study of human organizations are honest enough to admit it.

However, the Christian faith does not only provide a way of understanding. It provides a personal resource – that of Jesus Christ. The hidden treasure Christians have at their disposal is not just Christian theology; it is Christ himself. There are moments in reading modern business literature when one agrees entirely with the diagnosis but wants to cry out that there is an answer, a resource who is being sadly neglected. An example is the book by Roger Evans and Peter Russell, *The Creative Manager*, where they comment that in view of the pressures managers are under, one of the greatest needs of our time 'is to develop the capacity to be more at peace with ourselves; to find a still centre of inner stability and calm from which we can think and act with greater clarity and creativity'.[8]

While Christians do not have any monopoly on inner peace, many can testify that a personal relationship with Christ fills precisely the niche that Evans and Russell speak about. It is the wish to make an authentic Christian contribution to current debates about leadership which prompted the giving of the London lectures and the writing of this book.

2

Second Wave, Third Wave

The Complementary Arts
of Management and Leadership

Modern management literature is full of talk about corporate culture. It analyses the different styles of management and operating which permeate different companies. One of the most instructive discussions occurs in John Sculley's *Odyssey: Pepsi to Apple*,[1] a book which is a fascinating mixture of riveting autobiography and original analysis.

Sculley was Vice-President of Marketing at Pepsi during the 1970s, when he played a major role in raising Pepsi-Cola to the realm of corporate giants alongside Coca-Cola. Much to the surprise of his colleagues, Sculley was then lured away by Steve Jobs, the dynamic young founder of the up-and-coming Apple Computer Company, to become its Chief Executive Officer. It was a difficult decision to leave, but Jobs eventually persuaded Sculley to move by asking him the pointed question: 'Do you want to spend the rest of your life selling sugared water, or do you want a chance to change the world?'

In Apple, Sculley discovered a company with a culture diametrically opposed in almost every respect to that which he had experienced previously. At Pepsi, board meetings were elaborate in their formality and were a means of reinforcing the pecking order in the organization. At Apple, everyone dressed informally and arguments were wide-ranging and unpredictable. Apple too had a major corporate rival, IBM, but unlike Pepsi thought in terms of developing sharply differentiated products and of creating a whole new generation of customers. It was a major culture shock for Sculley, one that took time to get used to.

On reflection, Sculley came to understand the difference as one between *second wave* and *third wave* companies. The basic concept is one borrowed from Alvin Toffler,[2] but Sculley develops it in a distinctive way. He presents Pepsi as an outstanding example of the second wave (the industrial age), and Apple as an equally outstanding example of the third wave (the information age). They embody the series of contrasting management paradigms which can be seen in Table 1.

TABLE 1. **Contrasting Management Paradigms**

Characteristic	Second Wave	Third Wave
Organization	Hierarchy	Network
Output	Market share	Market creation
Focus	Institution	Individual
Style	Structured	Flexible
Source of strength	Stability	Change
Structure	Self-sufficiency	Interdependencies
Culture	Tradition	Genetic code
Mission	Goals/strategic plans	Identity/directions
Leadership	Dogmatic	Inspirational
Quality	Affordable best	No compromise
Expectations	Security	Personal growth
Status	Title and rank	Making a difference
Resource	Cash	Information
Advantage	Better sameness	Meaningful differences
Motivation	To complete	To build

Odyssey: Pepsi to Apple, p. 95

Most of the contrasts in the table are self-explanatory. By 'genetic coding', Sculley means an imprint of the company's identity which is evident in all that it does, but which may be expressed in a great variety of ways. Unlike tradition, it is forward looking. The genetic code at Apple consisted essentially in the vision of Steve Jobs: a society in which everyone was able to make use of a highly powered informational tool, the personal computer. In seeking to realize that vision, the company was engaged in a restless search to make its existing products obsolete as quickly as possible. The rate at which Apple enthusiasts in the 1990s change their computers shows how successful they are in this! Like other companies of its type, Apple is constantly seeking to present the customer with 'meaningful differences', which will prompt further purchasing.

Sculley thinks that though second wave companies have their strengths, third wave companies are the emerging form, not only for hi-tech companies, but for all institutions. This is because the source of their strength lies in their readiness for change. They are willing to adapt to changes in social habits, customer interests and the global economy. Their organization is highly flexible, often relying on a network of independent business partners.

Having gradually been won over to a third wave way of operating, John Sculley then experienced crisis two years after taking over at Apple. The company expanded rapidly during 1984 and 1985, but found itself piled high with computers it was unable to sell during 1986. This temporary loss of strategic direction was partly due to a deterioration in Sculley's relationship with Steve Jobs, an episode which ended with Jobs leaving the company. Sculley then realized that he had to act fast to save Apple.

When Sculley describes what he did to avert the crisis, it is striking how much he drew on his experience at Pepsi. He introduced a much more functional type of organization, appointing disciplined and experienced executives to the most important control jobs. He cut costs in a very decisive way, deeper than appeared necessary at the time; this involved closing a plant in Texas. For all his apparent conversion to a third wave style of company, Sculley acted in a second wave manner when crisis loomed. While he still invested boldly in research and development as a sign of his confidence in Apple's future, he imposed financial discipline on an organization which had begun to spend money like water.

During the six years since I first read that book, I have become aware of a number of lists by other authors which look rather like Sculley's. However, the distinction has not always been between different types of organization or culture; it has also been between the types of people who wield power or influence in the organizations. I have become conscious of a correlation between Sculley's second and third waves, and the respective arts of management and leadership.

The fact that there might be a significant difference between management and leadership was first brought home to me by a letter I received from the chairman of a leading firm of consulting engineers. This happened in the very early days of the Ridley Hall Foundation, when we were writing to companies and trying to attract interest in what we were doing. While the chairman said that he liked the sound of the Foundation, he expressed reservations about the prominence of the words 'manage' and 'management' in our literature. 'In our firm,' he said, 'we tend not to use the word management. We prefer leadership, which implies something more.'

Of the two terms, the title 'manager' is certainly found more widely in business, and the phenomenon of management has been analyzed in much more detail in the business literature. Peter Drucker is a well-known example of a business guru who has written book after book with 'managing' or 'management' in the title.[3] 'Management', he says, 'makes an organisation out of what would otherwise be a mob. It is *the* effective, integrative, life-giving organ.'[4] High praise indeed!

Something else I did early on at Ridley was to attend a

course at Sundridge Park Management Centre, on 'Principles of Effective Management'. Sundridge Park defines a manager as 'any person in any organization who is officially vested with the authority and accountability for directing and supervising the work of others.'[5] This takes in a lot of people: in Sundridge Park's estimation, about 2 million in this country. Managers are pretty thick on the ground, even if their numbers have been reduced in recent years by organizations which have decided that certain levels of management are a luxury they can no longer afford.

The State of the Debate

In recent years, however, there has been a growing interest in the subject of leadership. Two American gurus, James McGregor Burns and Warren Bennis, pioneered the way with their studies of leadership in the mid-1970s.[6] I shall return to their contributions shortly. In 1987, Walter Goldsmith, Chairman of Food for Britain, announced that 'Management is out of date now. We're talking about leadership. We've had too much management in this country and not enough leadership.'[7]

'Leaders' and 'leadership' chimed in with the new breed of entrepreneurs which characterized the 1980s. Where management seemed dull and plodding, leadership was dynamic and exciting. Nor was the term confined to people at the top of organizations. Groups on the shop floor acquired team leaders. The trend was not universal, but in some sectors of our corporate life leadership is all the rage and management is on the wane.

The cynic might say that this is simply a play on words, that the two activities are essentially the same thing, and that business writers are fooling a gullible public by pretending there is a significant distinction. Peter Drucker, in a robust little article called 'Leadership: More Doing than Dash', concludes that the skills of leadership are 'no different at all from what we have known for years are the requirements for being an effective manager'.[8] But I think there is a genuine difference. Moreover, there seems to be a growing consensus of opinion as to what are the characteristic activities of management, on the one hand; and leadership, on the other. Sundridge Park's characterization of the fourfold function of management, as *planning, organizing, controlling* and *evaluating*, is pretty typical. Leadership, in contrast, is about setting a direction and motivating others to follow: it is about *aligning* and *inspiring*.

In an interview in *Director* magazine, John Adair explored the etymological roots of the distinction between 'leading' and 'managing'. He said this:

> Leadership is about a sense of direction. The word 'lead' comes from an Anglo-Saxon word, common to north European languages, which means a road, a way, the path of a ship at sea. It's knowing what the next step is. . . . Managing is a different image. It's from the Latin *manus*, a hand. It's handling a sword, ship, a horse. It tends to be closely linked with the idea of machines. Managing has its origins in the 19th century with engineers and accountants coming in to run entrepreneurial outfits. They tended to think of them as systems.[9]

Warren Bennis made a similar distinction in his influential books *Leaders*, and *On Becoming A Leader*.[10] He coined a number of memorable aphorisms, for example: 'The manager has a short-range view; the leader has a long-term perspective'; 'The manager has his eye always on the bottom line; the leader has his eye on the horizon.' The most-cited of these aphorisms is: 'Managers are people who do things right and leaders are people who do the right thing.'[11]

In *Leaders*, Bennis and his co-author Burt Nanus argued that many organizations, especially the unsuccessful ones, are overmanaged and underled. The common characteristic of the successful leaders they studied was that their leadership was *transformative*. Such leadership creates a common social responsibility. It engenders people who 'buy into' a vision, know what needs doing and are happy to get on with it. Transformative leadership frees up and pools collective energies in pursuit of a common goal.

In using the language of transformation, Bennis acknowledges his indebtedness to the work of James McGregor Burns.[12] Burns argued that there were two sorts of leadership: transactional and transformational. Transactional leaders offer something tangible – such as jobs or financial benefits – in return for others' allegiance. Transformational leaders recognize that people have aspirations which go beyond these basic rewards, and offer a vision which unites leaders and followers in commitment to changing a situation for the better.

It is the enthusiastic adoption of a shared cause which lies at the heart of *empowerment*, another 'buzz' word in the organizational world in recent years. Leaders have confidence about giving people power to make significant decisions when they are sure that employees are keenly committed to the same ends. But the word 'empowerment' is misunderstood or used deceptively if it is held to mean that power has actually been given away. The reality almost always is that it has not. Robert Waterman gives an honest account of empowerment in terms of directed autonomy:

> In directed autonomy, people in every nook and cranny of the company are empowered – encouraged, in fact – to do things their way. Suggestions are actively sought. But all this takes place within a context of direction. People know what the boundaries are; they know where they should act on their own and where not. The boss knows that his or her job is to establish those boundaries, then truly get out of the way.[13]

Admittedly, the lengths to which empowerment can be taken, or the breadth of the boundaries within which employees are given freedom to operate, is something which will have huge cultural variants. Most of the literature cited above is American, and there is some evidence that these ideas translate less easily, say, to a southern than to a northern European context. For a leader to share power or delegate the responsibility of decision-making to others in certain Mediterranean countries is more likely to be seen as a negation of leadership than a positive step to empowerment.[14] But that does not mean that the concept is of no relevance; rather, that the appropriate expression for transforming and empowering leadership needs to be found for that cultural context.

An example of authority which has been devolved to an apparent extreme, within an organization that has been phenomenally successful, is *Maverick!*, the story of the Brazilian company Semco.[15] There, managerial staff set their own salaries and bonuses, everyone has access to the company books, and shop floor workers decide on their own productivity targets and schedules.

Many comments could be made about this, but I shall content myself with two. First, this radical experiment in industrial democracy was not put into operation overnight. It developed bit by bit, as one surprising innovation after another proved – against many predictions of doom – to be effective. Second, such a structure depends on employee goodwill and commitment to the corporate good. Employees in Semco have an extraordinary degree of freedom, but they make responsible decisions because they are genuinely concerned about the welfare of the organization, not just about feathering their own nest. The writer of *Maverick!*, Semco's owner Ricardo Semler, has clearly played a key role in evoking that commitment from the workforce. He may have discarded many of the conventional duties of management, but he has certainly exercised leadership.

Leadership in the Bible

Is the view that leadership has in essence a transforming function one which can be sustained from the Bible? This is not a straightforward question to answer. Leadership as such is not a concept that occurs in the Bible. But the responsibilities, privileges and temptations of power are themes on which the biblical writers meditate frequently.

Consider for instance three contrasting passages on the nature of kingship. The royal wedding song Psalm 45 extols the glories of the king in all his beauty and majesty, which reflect the special favour of God:

> You are the fairest of the sons of men;
> grace is poured upon your lips;
> therefore God has blessed you for ever. . .
> Therefore God, your God, has anointed you
> with the oil of gladness above your fellows;
> your robes are all fragrant with myrrh and aloes and
>   cassia
> *Psalm 45.2, 7–8*

Clearly this is kingship described in idealistic terms, but especially noteworthy is the fact that the king enshrines the highest of moral ideals. He is described as riding forth victoriously 'for the cause of truth and to defend the right' (verse 4). His royal sceptre is a sceptre of equity: 'you love righteousness and hate wickedness' (verse 6–7).

Psalm 45 affirms the material pleasures of the royal court, but Proverbs 31.1–9 casts a very different perspective. This comprises some highly practical, deeply humanitarian advice from the queen mother of Massa to her son Lemuel:

> It is not for kings, O Lemuel,
> it is not for kings to drink wine,
> or for rulers to desire strong drink;

lest they drink and forget what has been decreed,
and pervert the rights of all the afflicted.
Proverbs 31.4–5

Rather, drink should be given to those in distress, so that
they can forget their poverty and misery! Rulers should
not satisfy their self-indulgence, but speak out on behalf of
those who have no political voice: 'open your mouth, judge
righteously, maintain the rights of the poor and needy'.
The queen mother's advice therefore includes a recognition
of the temptations of power, and an insistence on the
responsibility of monarchs to create a fairer society.

There is also a severe warning, right at the start of the
monarchical period, about the likelihood of kings submit-
ting to the temptation to aggrandize themselves and abuse
others (1 Samuel 8). The Israelites came to Samuel demanding a king, looking to such a figure to transform their
political fortunes, but Samuel tells them bluntly that they
will live to regret the day they did so. In the hands of the
wrong individuals, power without checks and balances
spells oppression and exploitation: 'he will take the best of
your fields and vineyards and olive orchards and give them
to his servants. . .' (1 Samuel 8.14).

Many of the lessons which can be learnt about leadership from the Old Testament come through considering
the narrative sections of the Bible. The biblical writers
certainly have a strong emphasis on the *moral* dimension
of leadership, which I shall explore further in the next
chapter. But it is also possible to evaluate the achievement
of individual leaders in terms of the goals appropriate to
their particular historical situations, and how successful
they were in fulfilling them. Here one might say that
Moses – with spectacular divine support! – performed a
remarkable feat in leading the enslaved Israelites out of
Egypt, but somehow failed to inspire a wandering people
with the confidence that they could occupy the promised

land. Or, one could look at Nehemiah, who showed formidable leadership qualities in motivating a workforce to rebuild the walls of Jerusalem.[16] David is another example: his personal courage and charisma made him astonishingly successful in drawing people to fight under his banner (both for self and country), but inattention to the administration of justice made him vulnerable to the rebellion that was starting in his own family (2 Samuel 15).

Whatever the extent of their success, the ability to attract others to a worthwhile cause, align these followers in the same direction, encourage them to express their particular talents, and sustain a common vision in the face of considerable obstacles, are all qualities highlighted by stories about biblical leaders. They bear a close correspondence to the hallmarks of transforming leadership described by many contemporary writers. But the Bible is an assiduous recorder of the names and deeds of all types of people, and within the ranks of those who provided faithful support for the likes of Moses, David and Nehemiah there were doubtless many who performed a managerial function.

Integrating Management and Leadership

The business writer who, to my knowledge, has worked out the polarity between management and leadership in most detail is the American, Craig R. Hickman. In his book, *Mind of a Manager, Soul of a Leader*,[17] Hickman lists five key areas in corporate life:

- competitive strategy / advantage
- organizational culture / capacity
- external / internal change
- individual effectiveness / style
- bottom-line performance / results

In each of these areas he projects up to nine distinguishing characteristics between managers and leaders: a total of forty-four different polarities altogether. Hickman then works painstakingly through his list, giving examples from his experience as a business consultant of companies where unresolved tension between each of these polarities was the root cause of organizational difficulty or failure. Hickman's forty-four polarities can be seen in Table 2: Management and Leadership characteristics.

TABLE 2 **Management and Leadership Characteristics**

1. Competitive Strategy / Advantage

Managers	Leaders
Concentrate on strategies	Nurture cultures
Consider dangers	Sense opportunities
Follow versions	Pursue visions
Isolate	Correlate
Search for solutions	Identify problems
Service markets	Serve customers
Think rivals	Seek partners
Design incremental strategies	Lay out sweeping strategies
Correct strategic weaknesses	Build on strategic strengths

2. Organizational Culture / Capability

Managers	Leaders
Wield authority	Apply influence
Seek uniformity	Pursue unity
Administer programmes	Watch people
Formulate policies	Set examples
Instruct	Inspire
Manage by objectives	Manage by walking around
Control	Empower
Easily release people	Would rather keep people
Employ consistency	Elicit commitment

3. External / Internal Change

Managers	Leaders
Yearn for stability	Thrive on chaos
Duplicate	Originate
Fasten things down	Unfasten things
Drive toward compromise	Work to polarize
See complexity	See simplicity
React	Proact
Plan	Experiment
Reorganize	Rethink
Refine	Revolutionize

4. Individual Effectiveness / Style

Managers	Leaders
Ask how	Wonder why
Think logically	Think laterally
Perpetuate hierarchies	Strive for equality
Are sceptical	Are optimistic
Smooth	Confront
Take charge	Let go
Like formality	Prefer informality
Venerate science	Revere art
Perform duties	Pursue dreams

5. Bottom-Line Performance / Results

Managers	Leaders
Scrutinize performance	Search for potential
Are dependent	Are independent
Compensate people	Satisfy people
Conserve assets	Risk assets
Pursue the tangible	Seek the intangible
Inhabit the present	Reside in the future
Concentrate on short-term results	Seek long-term results
Want good	Demand better

Taken from Craig R. Hickman, *Mind of a Manager, Soul of a Leader.*
Reprinted by permission of John Wiley & Sons, Inc.

Even though I find it difficult to believe that corporate problems always take this form, the evidence of organizational life suggests that Hickman is on to something important. I accept his polarities as plausible in outline, if questionable in detail. From that basis, I shall proceed to make seven observations about management and leadership. Some of these are points made by Hickman himself; others go considerably beyond what he says.

1. Many people are a mixture of managers and leaders. This might seem like a blatant contradiction of Hickman, with his neat division between the two types, but the fact is that he does not state his thesis as crudely as his list might suggest. He describes 'manager' and 'leader' as metaphors representing two opposite ends of a spectrum. 'Manager' signifies the more analytical, structured, controlled and orderly end; 'leader' the more experimental, visionary, flexible, uncontrolled and creative end. But as with all spectra, somewhere in the middle is an area where it is difficult to distinguish one from the other.

Readers may care to work their way through Hickman's list, and tick themselves as being closer to one polarity or the other.[18] If you do, you will probably find that there is a fair degree of cross-over. Thank God that we do not conform simply to types; by dint of the creative work of the Holy Spirit, and the particular influences which have shaped our development, we are all complex, often unpredictable and gloriously unique human beings. Nevertheless, some generalized statements about ourselves may be valid. Most readers will find that there are significantly more ticks on one side of the list than the other. We *can* talk meaningfully about managers and leaders, but must beware of thinking of them as mutually exclusive types.

2. Managers and leaders need self-understanding. Working through such a list systematically may be a useful step towards knowing where we stand on the management-leadership spectrum. If we are to function effectively in our organizations, it is very important that we know and understand ourselves: our traits and tendencies, likes and dislikes, strengths and weaknesses. The value of psychometric tests as an aid to doing this is being increasingly recognized across a range of organizations.

Many readers will be familiar with the Myers-Briggs Type Indicator. Whatever questions there may be about the Jungian theory of psychological type which underlies Myers-Briggs, the indicator appears to have value in bringing to light those aspects of our personality which are dominant and those which are more dormant. Myers-Briggs explores human personality in terms of four polarities: Extraversion and Introversion (E/I); Sensing and Intuition (S/N); Thinking and Feeling (T/F); Judging and Perception (J/P).[19] I recently heard that tests which have been carried out on different varieties of clergy reveal that liberal catholics are most likely to be INFP, certain types of evangelical ESTJ, charismatics ENFP, members of the radical 'Sea of Faith' movement ISTJ, and the sort of liberals who rejoice in being both woolly and warm ESFP![20] If readers' known preferences coincide with a group of unfamiliar bedfellows, I can only say: don't worry about it – such categorization is not to be taken too seriously. What I had not come across until I read Hickman's book was an application of Myers-Briggs to different styles of management and leadership. He has a table listing and describing the sixteen possible different permutations. This is reproduced as Table 3: Management / Leadership Type Table.

To get an accurate result from these tests, it is worth doing the longer rather than the shorter form, and also to ask someone who knows you well to score on your behalf to balance your own perception against how others see you. Most people find that when the personality type emerges, they recognize the description given. It often makes them realize something significant about themselves of which they were hitherto only semi-conscious.

Another dimension of ourselves which is important to know about is how we operate in teams. Here the work on team roles done by Meredith Belbin can be very revealing.[21] It grew out of an observation made by investigators at Henley Management College, that the teams made up of the most talented individuals in the games played on management courses were seldom the most successful. A combination of different types in a team was much more crucial to effective functioning. Belbin's research then unearthed what these roles were. Through psychometric tests, it is possible to plot where one stands in terms of nine different roles: plant, resource investigator, co-ordinator, shaper, monitor-evaluator, teamworker, implementer, completer and specialist. These roles are characterized in Table 4: the Nine Team Roles.

For readers who are familiar with Belbin's work from a few years back, it is worth noting that he has changed some of the role names and also added an extra one. This table is particularly valuable because it identifies not only each team member's contribution, but also their 'allowable weaknesses'. (Myers-Briggs in contrast tends to be more indiscriminately affirming, paying insufficient attention to the drawbacks of each personality type.) The weaknesses Belbin describes may of course become not allowable if they assume an exaggerated form, or if the team lacks someone willing and able to play a compensating role.

3. Managers and leaders need to appreciate each other.
One effect of doing either of these tests in a working group is to highlight the particular contribution each individual has to make. If one particular individual is of a strikingly different type from the majority, the team may then be able to understand why they have been experiencing some tension (thereby taking some of the heat out of the conflict),

TABLE 3 **Management / Leadership Type Table**

ISTJ	ISFJ	INFJ	INTJ
Responsible Manager Does things right	**Accommodating Manager** Serves poeple	**Inspirational Leader** Inspires others	**Perfecting Leader** Improves everything
ISTP	ISFP	INFP	INTP
Solution Manager Addresses expedient needs	**Observant Manager** Is sensitive to all	**Idealistic Leader** Seeks to transform society	**Holistic Leader** Pursues logical purity
ESTP	ESFP	ENFP	ENTP
Realistic Manager Gets things done	**Enthusiastic Manager** Makes work enjoyable	**Opportunistic Leader** Discover possibilities	**Inventive Leader** Finds new insights
ESTJ	ESFJ	ENFJ	ENTJ
Achieving Manager Accomplishes objectives	**Facilitating Manager** Provides help	**Persuasive Leader** Articulates values	**Conquering Leader** Drives toward goals

Taken from Craig R. Hickman, *Mind of a Manager, Soul of a Leader.*

and also to appreciate that person's unique contribution rather better. I was once the member of a team of Js, with a chairman who was a P. Doing Myers-Briggs helped us to understand why our committee meetings felt slow-moving and indecisive. It also underlined the thoroughness with which the chairman explored all the possible options.

The same is true more generally with regard to managers and leaders. It is crucial for the manager to appreciate the gifts and person of the leader, and vice versa, because both have an invaluable role to play. To take an example from

TABLE 4 **The Nine Team Roles**

Roles and Descriptions – Team-Role Contribution	Allowable Weaknesses
Plant: Creative imaginative, unorthodox. Solves difficult problems.	Ignores details. Too pre-occupied to communicate effectively.
Resource investigator: Extrovert, enthusiastic, communicative. Explores opportunities. Develops contacts.	Overoptimistic. Loses interest once initial enthusiasm has passed.
Co-ordinator: Mature, confident, a good chairperson. Clarifies goals, promotes decision-making, delegates well.	Can be seen as manipulative. Delegates personal work.
Shaper: Challenging, dynamic, thrives on pressure. Has the drive and courage to over-come obstacles.	Can provoke others. Hurts people's feelings.
Monitor evaluator: Sober, strategic and discerning. Sees all options. Judges accurately.	Lacks drive and ability to inspire others. Overly critical.
Teamworker: Co-operative, mild, perceptive and diplomatic. Listens, builds, averts friction, calms the waters.	Indecisive in crunch situations. Can be easily influenced.
Implementer: Disciplined, reliable, conservative and efficient. Turns ideas into practical actions.	Somewhat inflexible. Slow to respond to new possibilities.

Completer: Painstaking, conscientious, anxious. Searches out errors and omissions. Delivers on time.

Inclined to worry unduly. Reluctant to delegate. Can be a nit-picker.

Specialist: Single-minded, self-starting, dedicated. Provides knowledge and skills in rare supply.

Contributes on only a narrow front. Dwells on technicalities. Overlooks the 'big picture'.

Strength of contribution in any one of the roles is commonly associated with particular weaknesses. These are called allowable weaknesses. Executives are seldom strong in all nine team roles.

Taken from R. Meredith Belbin, *Management Teams: Why They Succeed or Fail.*

each of Hickman's five areas: organizations need to consider dangers *and* to seek opportunities; to employ consistency *and* to elicit commitment; to refine *and* to revolutionize; to think logically *and* to think laterally; to conserve assets *and* to risk them. The leader needs to respect and value a manager's concern to protect the company's market share, and his skill at doing that. The manager should respect and value the leader's concern to identify new markets, and her skill at opening them up.

The two types, then, need each other. Paul's teaching in 1 Corinthians 12 about the church as a body (not one member but many, with each having an invaluable role to play) has its secular counterpart. Complementarity, not homogeneity, is the clue to organizational flourishing. But it is not enough simply to have members of a team who are different, and whose skills complement each other. Compliments as well as complements are in order! Each person must appreciate and value the contribution which

others provide, including those who are most unlike themselves.

**4. Managers and leaders need integrating into a cohe-
sive whole.** Integration is one stage further than coexistence, even mutually appreciate coexistence. It is a matter
of the whole being greater than a sum of the parts; of having the right people in the right place at the right time, all
working smoothly together. When I met the chairman of
the firm of consulting engineers who expressed distaste for
the word 'management', I discovered that his firm did in
fact have some managers. In that company, the concept of
management was confined to the handling of a particular
task, rather than seen as a more general function. Managers
were people appointed by the board of directors to oversee
specific projects. The directors themselves tended not to
be managerial types, but one of their key responsibilities
was to spot those who were.

There will be periods in an organization's history which
put a higher premium either on the qualities of leadership
or on the skills of management. The presence of a bold,
visionary leader, who believes passionately in his product
or service and can inspire others to follow in his wake, is
often crucial in the early stages of launching a company. I
recently met such a leader on the Cambridge Science Park.
The audacious aim of his little company is to become the
prime national alternative to BT for fixed phone services
throughout the UK, using radio rather than wire technology. I am sure that his gung-ho spirit played a major role
in his company being granted a licence to provide an alternative network by the Department of Trade and Industry.

But the entrepreneurial spirit cannot stand by itself.
Usually the indefatigable optimist needs to be comple-
mented by a hard-headed finance director, who can convince the bank or other lenders of capital that the leader's
dream is not just wishful thinking, and that the firm's
accounts are in safe hands. As I observed in chapter one,

once the company is up and running, it may also be appropriate in time for the entrepreneur to give way to someone who is more of a consolidator. This person is not someone lacking in imaginative qualities, but one who will build on what has been achieved, rather than launching out in a new direction too soon.

5. Managers are subordinate to leaders. This is not the same as saying that leaders are more important. The current fad that they are is misplaced. Managers repeatedly perform vital functions. For instance, there are many uncongenial but necessary tasks – such as unravelling a difficult technical problem, or breaking the news of redundancy to individuals – which are performed by managers rather than leaders. John Adair acknowledges that managers are often better than leaders at administration and control of financial resources.[22] When I am flying across the North Sea, and look out of the window thousands of feet above the sea, I sometimes think how vulnerable I and the other passengers would be if anything serious were to go wrong with the plane. But I am reassured by the knowledge that the engine mountings have been checked by a company with rigorous control systems – rather than by a company known for its experimentation and fluidity!

These essential management activities of planning, organizing, controlling and evaluating are therefore not optional extras. They need to be done. In the best sort of organization, as I argued earlier, all employees play a part in doing these things. They apply creative and critical thought to the work that they do, and thereby derive greater satisfaction from it. But managers need to take the initiative for ensuring such processes happen.

Nevertheless, the sort of activity I have in mind here is at the level of implementing a given policy; it is not that of setting a direction. The essence of leadership is that leaders *lead*. Others follow. There is therefore a sense in which the skills of management, crucial though they are, should be subordinate to the wider horizons of leadership. Leaders set the framework within which managers carry out their important tasks.

This distinction should not be interpreted in terms of status or importance, though the world's weary habits being what they are, inevitably it often is. The two roles are simply different, and should not be confused. Nor does it mean that the leader should be beyond criticism. Managers can often perform a valuable service to their organization when they question a leader's direction, or at least urge him or her to consider alternative possibilities. But so long as the leader remains in a position of authority in an organization, managers should pursue the direction set by the leader, rather than subvert the organization by pulling in the opposite one. The New Testament tells us to submit to those in authority, referring to leadership in society as much as in the church (for example, see Romans 13.1; 1 Peter 2.13–14).

When I gave my London lectures, this thesis that managers are subordinate to leaders came under question. It was suggested that in an organization with many highly creative individuals in senior positions, what was needed at the top was someone performing a strong management role, 'holding the ring' and not allowing any one individual's creative impulses to triumph at the expense of others. There may be truth in this, but I still believe that the person in the apex position needs to do more than play a maintenance or peace-keeping role. He or she needs to hold before people the corporate vision, to ensure that all these talented individuals are in fact drumming to the same tune. In an airline company, one dimension of this might be *enthusing* employees with the importance of observing safety requirements strictly; making rigorous control mechanisms a matter in which people take pride, and about which there are no short measures.

6. Leaders are not only found at the top of organizations. To say that managers should be subordinate to leaders might suggest that I have chairmen or chief executives chiefly in mind. I do have them in mind, but certainly not them alone! Two qualifications are in order. First, many large organizations are so complex that the heads of particular groups, regions or units are effectively leaders within that unit. While they report to leaders higher up the chain of command, they often have considerable freedom of action about what happens within their sphere of responsibility. Second, there are people with leadership qualities who pop up all over an organization. The gift of infectious enthusiasm is not limited to those in so-called leadership positions. Some people have it, others do not, but wherever it is present, and attitudes to work change as a result, leadership is being exercised. It is precisely through individuals taking the initiative and displaying such qualities that future leaders come to the fore and are identified.

In some organizations, there is actually a gulf between role and function: between the appearance of certain people holding leadership and management positions, and the reality whereby these functions are actually performed by others. The phrase 'power brokers behind the scenes' is often used in this context. Another is 'gatekeepers': people who have the knack of gathering information and passing it on. These are characters to whom others readily turn when they have questions about 'what?' and 'how?' Should the unofficial nature of their role be a matter for concern?

Two comments come to mind here. The first is that life is untidy, and it is unrealistic to expect the formal description of a management structure to conform precisely to what really happens. If unofficial leaders get things going, unofficial managers get things finished, and the organization fulfils its aims better as a result, why worry? The second is that such a gulf can become a problem if the disparity between appearance and reality becomes too large.

It could be an indication that authority in the organization is being flouted, that the wrong people are being promoted, or that gifted people are not receiving the recognition they deserve. Several of Jesus' parables encourage the conferment of more responsibility and opportunity on those who have proved they have 'got what it takes'.

7. Those who are not leaders benefit from understanding leadership better. In much of what follows I shall be concentrating on leadership rather than management. Those who consider themselves managers rather than leaders, or alternatively neither (and it is of course the third group, of followers or operatives, who will always constitute the largest portion of the workforce), may be tempted to think that the following chapters do not concern them. But this would be mistaken. If we are to appreciate leaders, see where they may be falling short and help them to be better leaders, we can all benefit by understanding more about leadership.

In any case, as I have said, the demarcation between leaders and others is not an absolute one. Leadership and management inevitably overlap. Many managers will find themselves required to exercise leadership qualities some of the time, even if the role does not come particularly naturally to them. Often we swop roles, both at work and between work and the other parts of our lives. Leadership repays careful thought on the part of all of us.

New Testament Images: Servant, Shepherd, Steward

In the New Testament, it is not only leaders like Jesus and Paul who catch the eye. It is the presence of certain striking and recurrent models or *images* of leadership. Arguably, there are three key images, all beginning with the letter 's': servant, shepherd, and steward.[23] Each of them is a rich image, replete with various connotations, and worthy of careful attention. I shall now seek to relate these three to what has already been said about management and leadership.

The prominence of the servant motif in the New Testament is well known. No one can dispute the authoritative position Jesus held among his disciples, and yet he said to them: 'I am among you as one who serves' (Luke 22.27). He gave a vivid example of this on the night before his death by washing his disciples' feet. This was the humblest of actions, yet it in no way diminished Jesus' authority. After the event he told them: 'You call me "Teacher" and "Lord", and you are right, for so I am' (John 13.13). In Philippians 2, Paul describes the whole saving initiative of Jesus Christ in terms of his taking the form of a *servant*: of emptying himself, being born in human likeness, humbling himself and becoming obedient, even to the point of death on a cross (Philippians 2.6–8).

At this point, the New Testament concepts of leadership might seem light-years away from the secular models which are espoused and practised today. To die upon a cross was excruciatingly painful and utterly humiliating. The word often used for 'servant' in the New Testament is *doulos*, more accurately translated as 'slave': it really does indicate a willingness to assume the lowliest of positions and endure hardship and suffering on behalf of other people. Jesus emphasized the gulf between his concept of leadership, and the notions of leadership which were current in his day, when he said these words: 'You know that those who are supposed to rule over the Gentiles lord it over them, and their great men exercise authority over them. But it shall not be so among you; but whoever would be great among you must be your servant, and whoever would be first among you must be slave of all. For the Son of Man came not to be served but to serve, and to give his life as a ransom for many' (Mark 10.42–5).

Without doubt, examples of a macho style of leadership

abound in the world today. But it is interesting to note that talk of 'servant leadership' is not confined to the church; it is cropping up in the business literature to an increasing extent. Where the notion of business as providing a service is taken seriously, it is only logical to apply that same willingness to serve to those who lead business organizations. In their recent book on leadership entitled *Credibility*, James M. Kouzes and Barry Z. Posner devote a chapter to the theme of service and say that 'serving others is the most glorious and rewarding of all leadership tasks'.[24] They pay tribute to a book written in 1977 by Robert Greenleaf, *Servant Leadership*.[25] Greenleaf was a Christian management consultant who became convinced from a lifetime's experience in industry that the principles of servant leadership really work in the secular world. He writes: 'the great leader is seen as servant first, and that simple fact is the key to greatness.'[26] He believes that the willingness of people to follow a leader is directly related to the extent to which his or her servant stature is clearly evident.

I have even come across the phrase, 'a good leader is one who is prepared to die for his organization'! While it is questionable whether most business organizations are worth that measure of sacrifice, there is no denying that good leadership involves denial of self and cost to self.

I suggest that this denial of self often takes one of two forms. The first consists in a willingness to delegate. It can be very difficult to delegate, especially when the task is something we rather enjoy, or when we know that the job will be done much better if we do it ourselves, rather than giving it to an employee who is attempting it for the first or second time. But we ourselves, the staff to whom tasks are delegated, and the organization as a whole, will all be better served in the long run if we are prepared to pass on certain responsibilities to others. A leader needs to conserve his or her energies by keeping *focused*, and not being distracted by sundry matters which can be taken care of perfectly well by others. If this involves taking a less public, more background and self-effacing role, so be it. Genuine servant leaders are happy for others to get the credit rather than themselves.

The second form of self-denial consists, paradoxically, in the complete opposite: an unwillingness to delegate. I should add to that sentence: 'the things that are the proper responsibility of the leader'. For instance, deciding on the shape and content of an organization's mission statement is not something a leader should simply leave to others. By all means, involve others in producing it, encourage as many people as possible in the organization to 'own' it, but if the mission statement is going to be worth anything at all, the leader must feel thoroughly comfortable with it and back it to the hilt. There is also that necessary assumption of responsibility, which a leader should be prepared to carry when the organization is under serious attack. It is cowardice, not delegation, to hide behind a publicity officer in those circumstances. The sense that 'the buck stops here' is part of the necessary cost of leadership.

Sometimes, also, there is a real place for self-sacrifice in terms of giving up some of the financial benefits and perks usually associated with positions of leadership. In a climate where cutting costs by making people redundant is the order of the day, there are a few examples of organizations where staff have foregone wage rises, or even accepted wage cuts, in order to reduce such cuts to a minimum. This is only likely to happen if the leader sets a strong visible example in terms of self-sacrifice. Nehemiah provides a good biblical example here: as governor of Judah, he refused certain privileges, notably a special food allowance, in order to reduce the financial burden on the ordinary people (Nehemiah 5.14–19). The self-serving tendencies of directors of recently privatized utility companies in contemporary Britain provide a striking contrast. Accepting pay rises well above the rate of inflation is

scarcely an encouragement to employees lower down the
line to observe pay restraint and thereby help to hasten
economic recovery.

Servanthood, then, is a very important biblical concept
for leadership, but it is not reserved only for those who are
leaders. Christians in general are 'servants of God' and are
expected to serve other people. A readiness to serve should
be characteristic of managers just as much as leaders. But
the power and status which are customarily associated with
leadership make the reminder of their servant function
particularly important for leaders.

Let us now turn to a New Testament image which *is*
used exclusively for leaders, that of the *shepherd*. Jesus is
described as both 'the good shepherd' (John 10.11), and
'the great shepherd' (Hebrews 13.20). In reinstating Peter
after the resurrection, Jesus tells him to do the work of a
shepherd (John 21.15–19). Peter in turn exhorts church
elders to be shepherds of God's flock (1 Peter 5.2), as does
Paul at Ephesus in Acts 20.28.

Again, one is conscious of a cultural gulf in applying
this image today. It is a strongly rural and agricultural
image, seemingly inappropriate to industrial and urban
settings. It has been distorted by sentimental religious
painting which presents the 'good shepherd' as a delicate,
rather effete figure. It also suggests a rather paternalistic
view of leadership, in which those who follow, the sheep,
are seen as weak, foolish and easily led astray. Yet if we
could recover a more accurate impression of what being a
shepherd in biblical times actually involved, some of these
problems would disappear.

In his book *Rediscovering Pastoral Care*, Alastair Campbell
has pointed out that shepherding was a demanding and at
times hazardous occupation. 'During the long dry season
it was necessary to move the flocks over considerable dis-
tances in search of good pastures; suitable resting places
and watering places had to be found; and danger lurked in

the shadows of valleys in the form of robbers and wild beasts.'[27] Being a shepherd demanded courage.

There is a graphic example of this in the book of 1 Samuel, when young David, anxious to convince King Saul that he is capable of fighting Goliath, cites his experience as a shepherd boy. 'Your Majesty,' David says, 'I take care of my father's sheep. Whenever a lion or a bear carries off a lamb, I go after it, attack it, and rescue the lamb. And if the lion or bear turns on me, I grab it by the throat and beat it to death . . . The Lord saved me from lions and bears; he will save me from the Philistines' (1 Samuel 17.34–7).

We know from Psalm 23 that the shepherd had a rod, probably a cudgel in his belt, for beating off attackers. In a modern organizational context, leaders may require similar courage in defending members of staff from unjust and damaging accusations. This demands a readiness to be generous in terms of giving time, emotional energy and pastoral support for the victim of attack, and a willingness to confront the false accuser.

The other piece of David's equipment was a staff, or crook, used to exercise control over the sheep and prevent them from wandering off into danger. The shepherd is ready to act firmly because he knows what is best for the sheep. But it is not a harsh rule: there are frequent Old Testament images of God as a shepherd gathering his flock in his arms (Isaiah 40.11), bandaging those that are hurt (Ezekiel 34.16), and leading them to a place of refreshment (Psalm 23). The image conveys ideas of tenderness, nurture and devotion; the good shepherd knows and cares for his sheep individually. In the case of Jesus, we are again reminded of the self-sacrificial depths this care involved: 'The good shepherd lays down his life for the sheep' (John 10.11).

Although the New Testament clearly uses this image for leaders in the church, the combination of qualities

required of the shepherd – those of courage, care, protection, discipline and establishing direction – are characteristics which are relevant and applicable to leadership more
widely. In particular, I suggest that the *directive* element in
the role of a shepherd may provide a useful corrective
against a tendency in some quarters to interpret the servant
concept in too passive a way.

A third New Testament image is that of *steward*. Stewards
crop up frequently in the parables of Jesus, where they are
associated with qualities of faithfulness, loyalty, business
acumen, and the ability to provide for those under them.
Jesus asks: 'Who then is the faithful and wise steward,
whom his master will set over his household, to give them
their portion of food at the proper time?' (Luke 12.42).
Paul describes himself and his colleagues not only as servants of Christ, but 'stewards of the mysteries of God' (1
Corinthians 4.1). A bishop is said to be 'God's steward'
(Titus 1.7). Peter tells us to use our gifts as 'good stewards
of God's varied grace' (1 Peter 4.10). The concept of
steward is one that tends to appeal to Christian business-
people, because the responsibility of managing God-given
resources is often taken as the basic theological rationale
for being in business – with some justification.[28]

It is interesting that later on in the parable from Luke
12, the steward is called a servant. The variation of title
emphasizes his dual relationship, both in possessing
authority and being under authority. It is the position of
household manager that Jesus has in mind, and this is
what 'steward' (*oikonomos*) most often meant in the Middle
Eastern world. It may well be that this is therefore an
image more appropriate for managers than leaders! Yet as
soon as one says that, one must qualify it, because the
essence of stewardship is accountability: being accountable
to one's master for the management of resources. Leaders
too are accountable, though exactly who they answer to
varies widely, depending on their particular position and

the type of organization for which they work. To some extent, they are accountable to all the different groups to whom the organization bears responsibility, such as shareholders for the use of capital, and customers or clients for the quality of service. Leaders have been given much in terms of power, influence and resources, and Jesus' use of the steward image makes it clear that of those to whom much has been given, much is expected. This is true both on an earthly and a heavenly level. There is an eternal perspective. A Christian appraisal of leadership cannot avoid the challenging thought that in the final resort, leaders are answerable, not just to company chairmen, investment analysts or any other human grouping, but to God.

3

Wise as Serpents, Innocent as Doves

Leading with Integrity

Companies in the 1990s are increasingly into the business of articulating their core beliefs and aspirations. Some call these statements 'expressions of corporate philosophy', some call them 'mission statements', others 'expressions of general business principles'. They vary a great deal in form, but there is a similarity in content which runs through the majority of them. Statements of company philosophy articulate the values which the company seeks to embody (such as quality, mutuality, efficiency) and spell out the responsibilities which the company acknowledges towards various groups (such as shareholders, customers, employees).

This phenomenon is not limited to the commercial sector. It is increasingly common in the public sector, voluntary organizations, schools and so on. I even know of the occasional church which has a mission statement, though there are not too many of these! It is one of life's ironies that the movement which gave the world the word 'mission' tends to lag behind others when it comes to giving a clear account of what it exists to do.

Over the last few years, I have collected a considerable number of mission statements. Comparing them is an instructive exercise. There is one word which crops up with intriguing regularity. It is the word 'integrity'. Examples of these mission statements can be seen in Table 5.

TABLE 5 **Excerpts from Company Mission Statements**

Cadbury Schweppes – We should set high standards and expect to be judged by them. The quality we aim for in all our dealings is that of integrity.

National Westminster Bank – Our first priority is integrity in our dealings as a financial services institution . . . The NatWest group is committed to building and maintaining high standards of integrity, fair dealing, quality of service and ethical behaviour in all its relationships.

Ford Motor Company – Integrity is never compromised. The conduct of our company world-wide must be pursued in a manner that is socially responsible and commands respect for its integrity and for its positive contributions to society.

British Petroleum – We are committed at all times to integrity and fairness, to quality products and services which give our customers good value.

London Buses – All employees shall seek to uphold and enhance the standing of the company by maintaining an unimpeachable standard of integrity in all their business relationships.

Shell – Shell companies insist on honesty and integrity in all aspects of the business.

Hewlett-Packard – We conduct our business with uncompromising integrity. People at every level are expected to adhere to the highest standards of business ethics and must understand that anything less is totally unacceptable.

United Biscuits – Our reputation for integrity is the foundation on which mutual trust between the company and its customers is based. We expect compliance with our standard of integrity throughout the company, and we will support an employee who passes up an opportunity or advantage which can only be secured at the sacrifice of principle.

British Aerospace – Care must be taken in the selection of agents and consultants who should be persons of the highest integrity.

These statements involve grand and far-reaching claims. I know the former occupant of a very senior position at Ford who confessed to being quite awestruck by his company's claim: 'Our integrity is never compromised.' But what do these wonderful aspirations mean in practice? This is a question to which I shall return shortly.

Integrity and the Bible

It is worth drawing attention to the fact that the word 'integrity' is also found, quite frequently, in the Bible. More precisely, it is found in a particular part of the Bible, the writings in the middle of the Old Testament known as the wisdom literature.[1] In Job 2.3, the Lord says to Satan: 'Have you considered my servant Job, that there is none like him on the earth, a blameless and upright man, who fears God and turns away from evil? He still holds fast his integrity . . .' A few verses later, Job's wife utters these spine-chilling words: 'Do you still hold fast your integrity? Curse God, and die' (Job 2.9).

Job of course refrains from following her advice. In Job 27.5, he replies to his critics: 'Far be it from me to say that you are right; till I die I will not put away my integrity from me', and in Job 31.6 he makes the bold plea: 'Let me be weighed in a just balance, and let God know my integrity.' In Job, integrity clearly indicates an upright, righteous standard of behaviour, though perhaps there is a hint of something more. Part of Job's integrity was a searching honesty which refused to acknowledge fault where he believed no fault existed.

There are several instances of 'integrity' in the Psalms, where it is often used as a parallel word for righteousness or uprightness (for example, Psalm 7.8 and 25.21). Psalm 26 uses the word twice. It first appears in verse 1: 'Vindicate me, O Lord, for I have walked in my integrity.' Then, after pointing up a contrast with 'men in whose hands are evil devices, and whose right hands are full of bribes', the plea is made: 'But as for me, I walk in my integrity; redeem me, and be gracious to me' (verse 11). Twice the psalmist strikes the note of *walking* in one's integrity. The picture intended is perhaps that of a path or channel, a settled groove within which the good man operates, or of a godly ambience or atmosphere which surrounds everything he does. Integrity becomes the air you breathe or the ground you tread.

The book of Proverbs also provides some interesting examples of 'integrity'. In Proverbs 11.3: 'The integrity of the upright guides them, but the crookedness of the treacherous destroys them.' Here the implication is that integrity contributes to one's success. However, even if it brings no financial reward, Proverbs 19.1 insists: 'Better is a poor man who walks in his integrity than a man who is perverse in speech, and is a fool.' Integrity, in contrast, presumably has something to do with plain speaking.

A rare use of the word in another part of scripture occurs in Genesis 20. This is the curious story where Abraham, staying rather apprehensively in Gerar, pretends that his wife Sarah is his sister, with the consequence that Abimelech king of Gerar takes her. God then comes to Abimelech in a dream, and says, 'Behold, you are a dead man, because of the woman whom you have taken; for she is a man's wife.' Abimelech replies that he has been misled, and protests, 'In the integrity of my heart and the innocence of my hands I have done this.' God then relents, on condition that Abimelech restores Sarah to her husband, because (as God says), 'I know that you have done this in the integrity of your heart.' 'Integrity' here seems to mean something like sincerity: acting with pure intentions, without malice or guile.

Integrity as High Moral Standards

From studying the biblical material, and analysing the way we use 'integrity' in a contemporary context, I would now like to spell out some implications of this rich word. I believe that this process of teasing out needs to be done by all the organizations which trumpet their claim to integrity so readily. It could be a very instructive exercise, revealing just how much moral consensus exists within an organization.

First of all, integrity implies high moral standards. Fair dealings, vigilance over standards of quality and safety, and respect for the law all come to mind here. But integrity is particularly associated in people's minds with the quality of *honesty*. In their book *Credibility*, Kouzes and Posner refer to extensive international research done among employees about the characteristics they most admire in leaders.[2] Integrity is one of the three most cited characteristics, and for most employees it means beings honest – a habit of being straight with people, so that they know where they stand.

However, although being honest is a quality which is widely prized, it is equally often notable by its absence. It sounds an easy enough thing to do, but the reality of experience belies this. The temptation to cover up underhand deals, personal mistakes, and unwelcome news in the workplace is a strong one, for the leader just as much as anyone else. Honesty can be costly, but there is no doubt that it is a trait which is generally appreciated. Honesty breeds an atmosphere of trust.

Another important aspect of integrity is *consistency*. Leaders who are consistent do not surprise too many people with their moral decisions. Having set out their stall, they stick by it. They do not say one thing one day and something radically different the next.

In this respect, we can learn as much from those we have come to recognize as bad leaders as from the good. A leader who makes arbitrary decisions spreads confusion and fear among the ranks. Biographies written about Robert Maxwell since his death show that he was a notorious example of this. He delighted in making unexpected decisions as a way of keeping people on their toes and in his thrall.[3] A more horrifying, because murderous, example is SS Hauptsturmführer Amon Goeth, whose reign of terror among the Jewish community in Krakow has become famous through the book and the film *Schindler's List.*[4] If, when he had been appointed, Goeth had simply lined up all the Jews and shot the lot of them, it would arguably have been less cruel than what he did. Goeth would shoot people quite arbitrarily, without any discernible rhyme or reason, acting on violent whims which kept the subject community in a terrifying state of insecurity. These bad examples serve to highlight how the leader with integrity, the person who is consistent, has in contrast a *reassuring* effect on his or her staff.

A further dimension of integrity, which has been the subject of less attention than the others, is *public defensibility.* By this I mean that the person or organization with integrity is willing and able to explain controversial actions without embarrassment in public. It is a mark of the leader with integrity that he or she is, generally speaking, prepared to make an open profession. Such a profession may not convince everyone, but the readiness to come forward and make a plausible case, and answer questions from potential critics, is surely laudable. 'Straight' behaviour of this type is good for internal morale, as well as for external reputation.

Integrity as Integration: Wholeness of Character

The concept of integrity should not be reduced simply to the qualities just outlined, or even the sum total of them. Integrity is more than that. Robert Solomon, the author of *Ethics and Excellence,* writes this: 'Integrity is not so much a virtue itself as it is a complex of virtues, the virtues working together to form a coherent character, an identifiable and trustworthy personality.'[5] Integrity suggests, logically enough, a life that is well integrated. There is a coherence between the different parts of it. The value systems professed by the person or organization concerned are adhered to in all areas of life, public and private.

At this point it is difficult to avoid reference to the thorny area of sex. A company chairman who preaches scrupulous loyalty to one's word in every business transaction, shows a lack of integrity if at the same time he is breaking his marriage vows by carrying on an adulterous affair with a colleague's wife. In the Old Testament, King David had many virtues as a leader, but the lack of discipline and order in his private life (and I am thinking of his failings as a father as much as his affair with Bathsheba) was a running sore which makes one hesitate to ascribe integrity to him. At the present time, the well-publicised amorous adventures of several leading Conservative MPs appear to have been a contributory factor in the party's loss of public respect and confidence in their fitness to govern.

A leader with integrity is well integrated. There is a *togetherness* about his or her personality. The secular world might describe it as wholeness of character. Christians might go further and call it holiness of character. Whichever epithet you prefer, there are few higher compliments you can shower on someone than to say they are a person of integrity.

The idea of integrity as togetherness is also worth considering in a corporate or social context. I have heard the suggestion from an Old Testament specialist that integrity or wholeness could be an alternative rendering of the Hebrew word *shalom*, which is usually translated 'peace'. Psalm 85 is a good example of a biblical passage which looks forward to a time when heaven and earth will be in perfect partnership:

Love and faithfulness meet together;
righteousness and peace kiss each other.

Faithfulness springs forth from the earth,
and righteousness looks down from heaven.
The Lord will indeed give what is good,
and our land will yield its harvest.
Righteousness goes before him
and prepares the way for his steps.
Psalm 85.10–13

This is integrity in an ultimate sense: God and human
beings acting together in harmony, with the human qualities of faithfulness and peace responding to the divine
attributes of love and righteousness. Both the psalmist's
and the prophets' vision of *shalom* means much more than
a mere absence of war. It is a state of concord which is
grounded on right relationships vertically (between God
and people), and right relationships horizontally (between
different people). In passages like Isaiah 11.6–9, even
relationships with and within the animal kingdom are
affected.

The reference to abundant harvests in Psalm 85.12 is
worth noting. *Shalom* includes the idea of abundance. The
church today routinely prays for peace and justice, but
rarely for the creation of economic conditions which help
such qualities to flourish. For someone immersed in the
world of business, however, perhaps the opposite caution
is needed. There the desirability of a state of prosperity is
taken as second-read. The importance of justice, peace, and
rooting both in a right relationship with God, are much
more likely to go by default. But the leader with integrity
is concerned about such things, because he or she knows
that they belong together and feed off each other.

Problems: Flawed Personalities

At this point, however, I want to stop in my tracks and
listen to some obvious objections. Integrity is all very well
as an ideal, you may say, *but*. Precisely. We need to take the

force of that *but*. It is time to step back for a moment from these statements of lofty ideal (not abandoning them, but stepping back), and infuse the discussion with some solid realism. This realism is needed in three different, interrelated areas.

First of all, we need to be realistic about ourselves. The fact of the matter is this: that though most of us are hopefully making some progress in the Christian life, we are not as well integrated as we would like to be. We suffer from flawed personalities. I have in fact felt slightly uncomfortable pointing the finger at bad examples of leadership earlier, because I am very conscious that 'there but for the grace of God go I'. When we read the Sermon on the Mount and come under the searching spotlight of the words of Jesus, we become aware of the many ways in which we fall short, and of the foibles and inconsistencies which mar our lives.

We may believe wholeheartedly in the virtues of kindness, patience and good humour, and then bewilder others and disappoint ourselves by giving vent to a sudden, uncontrolled loss of temper. We may believe profoundly in the sanctity of marriage and the dignity of woman, and then find ourselves irresistibly drawn to some pornographic material which we stumble across unexpectedly. We may believe implicitly that love and justice are universal imperatives which should be practised towards everyone, and then find ourselves consumed with loathing or prejudice towards someone who is the exact antithesis of us in every way. We fall short, sometimes a long way short, of our highest hopes and aspirations.

Last year, a visiting speaker came to Ridley Hall and did a very interesting exercise with some of our ordination students. First he asked them to share some of the things they hoped to see happening in the churches to which they would shortly be going. The answers were predictably worthy: people growing in faith, a high level of mutuality

and interdependence in relationships, a manifestation of
the gifts and fruit of the Spirit, a community which had
an open, welcoming attitude to outsiders, etc. Then he
asked them to make a list of *saboteurs* – the things inside
them that might sabotage or frustrate the fufilment of
these high aspirations. They came up with the following:
a yearning for power; doing the right thing for the wrong
reason; wanting to be noticed; the desire to be popular
with everyone; avoiding conflict at all costs; dwelling on
one's own inadequacies; interpreting everything as an
attack on oneself.

The point is clear, and it applies just as much to leadership in the secular world as leadership in the church.
There are all sorts of baggage knocking around in our
inner psyche which can get in the way of realizing our fine
objectives. There are forces of disintegration which stand
in the way of our becoming the rounded, well-integrated
person that is the subject of our dreams.

There is no simple remedy to this problem. Our speaker
at Ridley was an expert in Jungian depths psychology, and
there were insights from that area which rang bells and
proved helpful for some of our students. Christians rejoice
in the possibility of repentance, the assurance of forgiveness, and the healing work of the Holy Spirit. We can
learn techniques of managing stress, avoid places of obvious temptation, and search for positive qualities in people
we find difficult to like. Through the experience of being
loved – by God and by other people – we become better
equipped to love other people. We relate to them neither
aggressively nor defensively, but with that appropriate
balance of confidence and humility which is again characteristic of the person with integrity. In short, we can be
healed; we can get better.

But in this life the healing is never total, the two steps
forward are often punctuated by at least one step backward.
We need to be honest about our failings and vulnerabilities,

and the fact that integrity remains an ideal to which we constantly aspire but never quite achieve. Alastair Campbell rightly says: 'The person of integrity is first and foremost a critic of self, of tendencies to self-deception and escape from reality, of desire for a false inner security in place of the confrontation with truth which integrity demands.'[6]

Problems: Intractable Organizations

Second, we need to be realistic about the organizations for which we work. The fact is that most corporate cultures settle for something less than the fine ideals they proclaim in public. Mission statements can have the feel of empty shells or hollow promises where there is a major gulf between what the organization says and what it does. Usually, however, this does not mean openly flouting the company code. It is more a case of diluting it, qualifying it, taking one's lead from something rather different: the prevailing culture of the part of the organization in which one works.

There are many practices which take place in working life which fall short of the standards of integrity outlined above, but are well-established customs nonetheless. Small groups often conspire to cheat their own organization. Manual workers know how to drag their feet over a particular task in order to earn extra money working overtime. Managers collaborate in making unreasonable claims for expenses on trips abroad. Organizations get wise to these tricks, of course, but people are adept at coming up with new ones, and where there is group solidarity in pursuing and defending a dishonest wheeze, they can be very difficult to root out.

In his book *Moral Mazes*, the American sociologist Robert Jackall investigated the occupational ethics which managers practise at work.[7] He observed what actually went on, down at the desk or out in the field, rather than paying too much attention to the ethical stances publicly professed by the company. The results were very revealing. His book portrays a world in which managers are pursued by an all-consuming desire for promotion, and a nagging anxiety about how they are viewed by those who matter in the company. They therefore become adept at manipulating appearances and hiding their true thoughts and feelings in the interest of 'getting on' – the practice of ensuring that you get the credit when things go well, and avoid the blame when they don't.

Jackall thinks that in such a climate the principal managerial virtue becomes an essential, pervasive and thoroughgoing *pragmatism*. He relates two incidents in the companies he investigated of individuals who made moral protests about dubious practices. One, who worked in a company's medical department, sought to draw senior managers' attention to the fact that most of the textile workers had suffered substantial hearing loss as a result of the high level of noise experienced in the mill. The other was a company accountant who came across a number of financial irregularities – bribery payments, doctored invoices, and misappropriation of pension funds – in the course of his work.

Both found themselves treated with a mixture of indifference and hostility; one decided to leave his company and the other was fired. The latter came to the sad conclusion: 'What is right in the corporation is what the guy above you wants from you. That's what morality is in the corporation.'[8] When Jackall interviewed others in the organizations about the fate which befell these individuals, they expressed very little sympathy. They saw the violations which upset the company whistleblowers as commonplaces of corporate life. Even when they acknowledged that matters of principle were involved, they thought business was all about trade-off between principle and expediency.

There was a ready acceptance that, in this trade-off, expediency usually wins.

One must beware of taking Jackall's sample as representative of corporate cultures everywhere. There are organizations which make conscious efforts to encourage individuals with moral scruples to make their disquiet known.[9] But even when objecting to an established practice may serve to improve one's standing in the eyes of those in a more senior position, the alienating effect it may have on relations with one's peers can still be very inhibiting. Few people like being unpopular, and in general, popularity *per se* is an aid to personal advancement.

The result of all this is that it can be hard for the person with genuine integrity to rise to the top of an organization. How hard will depend on many variable factors, such as the size and nature of the organization, who they know in positions of influence, and the qualities they exhibit as well as integrity. But as I said earlier, taking a moral stand can be costly. The person with integrity who aspires to leadership needs to consider subtle questions about how to avoid a 'holier than thou' attitude – in other words, how to make integrity attractive. He or she also requires wisdom about selecting the issues on which to take a stand. It is possible to get some dubious practices out of proportion, and it is better to save one's nervous energy for matters where some really important principle is at stake.

Fortunately, not all corporate cultures are intractable. I know someone who rose to be vice-chairman of a major bank who was given a brief to maintain the moral standards of the organization. Insider dealing and Third World debt were two issues in which he became particularly involved.[10] In the eyes of many, he came to personify the corporate conscience, and when he retired, the new chief executive made a point of discussing who should replace him in that role. It is an encouraging example, and one that gives rise to the thought that many organizations might benefit by taking ethical expertise and sensitivity into account in working out a balanced board of directors.

Problems: Complex Situations

The third area in which realism is needed is in relation to the complexity of life's situations. There are a whole host of circumstances which make acting out integrity difficult. The effect is that leaders with integrity end up feeling compromised, or their image as a person of integrity becomes more ambiguous than they would like it to be.

Consider again the matter of honesty. The moral requirement to be honest does not mean that we are always obliged to play a fully open hand. There is information which it is right to protect from disclosure for a variety of reasons: in order to preserve confidentiality, for instance, or to protect a competitive position. In the words of Ecclesiastes 3.7, there is 'a time to keep silence, and a time to speak'.

Consider again the matter of consistency. The moral obligation to be consistent does not mean that we have to adopt a 'wooden' approach, or constantly resort to the rule-book. We need to be flexible in our handling of individuals and situations, taking note of what is dissimilar about them as well as what is similar. A good leader understands what makes different people 'tick', identifying one person who might benefit by being set a really testing assignment, and another who needs an easier ride at present because of tensions in his relationship with wife and family. It is not inconsistent – though it may look like it – to make different demands upon the two.

Consider again the matter of public defensibility. The moral virtue of coming clean in public needs to be balanced by an awareness of the way information in the public domain is liable to be treated. It may be misused, quoted out of context and sadly distorted. The danger of the media doing this needs to be weighed against the damage which may also be done through not making any public statement at all.

So these issues are not simple. Ethical complexity is all around us. Leading with integrity is often a matter of walking through a moral minefield.

Improper Payments

I want to explore this complexity with respect to the vexed issue of improper payments. A blanket word for improper payment is 'bribe', which the *New Dictionary of Christian Ethics* defines as 'an inducement improperly influencing performance of a public function meant to be gratuitously exercised'.[11] But what exactly counts as improper? There are a number of different types of financial transaction which warrant consideration.

First, there is the extravagant gift or offer of hospitality, the sports car, crates of whisky, or a holiday in the Mediterranean – all of which are designed to make the person who accepts them feel that he owes the giver something in return. In this country there is a widely respected convention that such gifts are acceptable only on a distinctly modest level. A typical company policy, though one stated more clearly and fully than most, is that found in British Gas's Code of Conduct (see the box). Gifts 'of a trifling nature' are commonly thought to mean calendars, diaries and pens. The implicit statement that gifts of a more substantial nature may be permissible in an international setting is interesting, and something to which I shall return shortly. The other box contains Hewlett-Packard's Standards of Business Conduct.

I have no particular difficulty with these statements, other than to observe that some of the practices they describe are, by their very nature, ambiguous. For instance, 'enhancing a business relationship' is a subtle process. I

British Gas Code of Conduct

Sensitive Payments

The registration of British Gas plc under US Securities laws means that British Gas is subject to the US Foreign Corrupt Practices Act 1977 (FCPA) in relation to its worldwide activities.

The FCPA makes it a crime to pay or give anything of value, directly or through an intermediary to any foreign official, foreign political party or candidate for foreign political office where the purpose is to assist the payer or donor in obtaining, retaining or directing business by (1) influencing a decision by the payee or donee or (2) inducing him/her to use his/her influence. Heavy penalties apply for violation of these provisions, both in terms of fines imposed, and in the case of individuals, to periods of imprisonment.

Gifts, Hospitality or Benefits

It is a criminal offence to accept or solicit any gift or consideration from anyone as an inducement or reward for showing favour in connection with British Gas's business.

To avoid any possibility of misunderstanding, all such offers other than gifts of a trifling nature should be politely but firmly declined. Similarly, employees should not send any gift, other than British Gas promotional items, to anyone employed by an outside organisation, Government Department or Local Authority or anyone else with whom British Gas has or may have a business relationship. The exception to this is where during the normal course of doing business in the international field, the customs and circumstances require the offering of business gifts to Foreign Government officials and business associates. The offer and acceptance of gifts in such circumstances should be in line with formal policies of Exploration and Production or Global Gas.

Any approaches from contractors, suppliers or traders, seeking favoured treatment in consideration of any offers of benefits or hospitality must be firmly declined and the circumstances reported to the Controller of Group Audit.

Business entertainment should be on a reciprocal basis and on a scale consistent with that which you, when host, would be authorised to arrange.

> If an employee has the slightest doubt about accepting any offer of benefits, they have clearly recognised a potentially dangerous situation and should seek guidance from their immediate manager who may consult the Controller of Group Audit.

Hewlett-Packard Standards of Business Conduct

> HP employees and members of their immediate families may not accept any gift, payment, loan or other favour from an HP customer, supplier or competitor.
>
> Employees may accept inexpensive advertising novelties. Care should be exercised in the acceptance of business lunches, dinners and entertainment. Such activities should be infrequent, consistent with accepted business practices, and for the express purpose of enhancing a business relationship.
>
> Advertising novelties, favours and entertainment may be given to customers and suppliers at HP expense only if: (a) they are consistent with accepted business practice; (b) they are of limited value and cannot be construed as a bribe or pay-off; (c) they do not violate any law or generally accepted ethical standards; and (d) public disclosure of the facts will not embarrass HP.

think what Hewlett-Packard mean is getting to know someone better, with the result of being able to make a more informed decision about doing business with them. But business decisions are inevitably affected by questions of interpersonal chemistry and warmth of friendship. In the development of close and trusting relationships, acts of generous hospitality are bound to play a part. If I have been invited to join a potential business partner for a day's golf and find the experience enjoyable, my commercial judgement is likely to be affected, whether I intend that it should be or not. I see no need to take an ascetic approach and deny all such experiences – I am too much of a golf addict for that! However, it is important to be aware how the dynamics of a relationship work.

Second, there is the type of payment best described as extortion. An official demands a payment in order for a routine service to be performed. You want to get your freight unloaded? You give the customs official something. Your organization wants a telephone line installed? You pass a suitable sum over the counter. Your company wishes to have a loan from the bank? You make it financially advantageous to the bank manager.

Such examples sound shocking, and fortunately they are rare in Britain. But there are other parts of the world where extortionate demands are everyday practice. Several could be mentioned. I am particularly aware of the problems of doing business in Central and Eastern Europe, through my involvement in a consultation entitled 'Integrity in Business' which was organized by two inter-denominational Christian research foundations.[12] It took place in Kocovce, Slovakia, in March 1994. There were twenty of us present, with a combination of Central and Eastern Europeans (the Czech Republic, Slovakia, Poland, Hungary, Romania and Bulgaria were all represented), westerners working in those countries, and people who live in the West. There was a good mix of business practitioners, and academics interested in business.

This was a memorable conference. One evening we sat round a blazing log fire, drinking wine and listening to the Eastern Europeans sharing stories about the heady days of late 1989, when Communism fell. The fact is, of course, that not everything has been plain sailing since then, and this was exactly what the consultation was concerned to explore: the problems of doing business (or getting business moving) in cultures dominated by prohibitive levels of taxation, a poorly developed work ethic, inadequate foreign investment, and corruption in many places. Extortionate payments are the order of the day. I have since heard of the difficulty experienced by a Polish participant in the conference when he subsequently attended another

conference in Prague. He changed Polish money into
Czech in advance of his trip, only to be told at the border
crossing that this was not permitted. He had to leave the
money with the official. He was then given a document
which revealed that he would only be given 10 per cent of
the money back on his return.

While such a level of extortion is clearly excessive, some
people defend the asking and giving of more modest payments as an alternative way of rewarding service. Some call
them 'customary payments', others – particularly Americans
– call them grease. Their essence is that they do not confer
special privileges, they are expected of everyone, and they
are regarded as a legitimate means of augmenting small
incomes in certain countries. If the officials concerned
were paid a decent salary, so it is argued, they would not
be necessary.

There is a certain force in this argument, and I would
not criticize my Eastern European friends who felt they
had no option but to make these payments in certain con-
texts. But all of us at the conference felt strongly that this
is a far from satisfactory method of operating. One of the
Slovakians present said that he would far rather pay extra
to have a telephone fitted if the money was going to the
company (who might then be able to pay their staff better),
than if it was going straight into an official's pocket.
Where additional payments go undeclared, there is clearly
scope for embezzlement on a massive scale. Asking for an
official receipt is one way of registering concern that a payment should be put on a proper public footing. Even if, in
exceptional circumstances, one accedes to an extortionate
demand, it is surely important to protest about it. While
protests can seem futile and empty gestures, they have sig-
nificance as a moral witness to a different way of behaving.
If the protests are loud enough and pervasive enough, they
can sometimes succeed in wearing a system down.

I cannot pretend that our consultation in Slovakia will

have had any dramatic effects in changing the overall situation. But it did produce a stiffening of resolve on the part of Christians working in Eastern Europe to build up *communities of resistance*: recognizing that they could not act with entirely clean hands, but trying to create islands of integrity where business is conducted on a different footing. Their hope is that in due course the ripples of such activity will spread wider throughout society. Such people need our prayers. Western organizations have a choice about whether to operate in such countries; they do not.

Extortion actually comes in both a 'soft' and a 'hard' form. The soft form is that if payment is not forthcoming, nothing happens. The expected service does not materialize. The hard form is that if payment is not forthcoming, unpleasant things happen. Physical violence is threatened, or blackmail. This is certainly a form of extortion that it is impossible to justify; but it is clearly a form of extortion which only moral heroes succeed in resisting. The tales of what was going on in Slovakia, Poland and Hungary paled into insignificance besides the horror stories that were coming out of Russia, where the Mafia has taken over large parts of the country and is practising, not a free market economy, but an intimidation and protection racket economy. Bank managers have been shot for refusing to reveal details of their customers' accounts.

Third, there is the type of payment most readily associated with the word 'bribe'. The essence of this is that it secures the payer a benefit which is thereby denied to anyone else. Hence the phrase which is sometimes used: 'special payment'. Many people pass through customs controls; only one company, normally, wins a particular contract. Putting money in the pocket – or more likely the Swiss bank account – of the government minister who decides the destination of a contract is an unfair way of securing competitive advantage.

In Slovakia, a major multinational oil company was finding it impossible to make any headway in setting up petrol stations, because a rival Austrian company persistently paid bribes in order to get planning permission from local government authorities. Being true to its professed corporate policy of integrity is therefore proving costly for the Company in that context. In the long run, however, the greater cost is probably being borne by the countries that tolerate and encourage such practices. If Eastern Europe had less of a climate of bureaucratic corruption, it would be far more attractive to foreign investors.

The way in which contracts are often secured in other parts of the world, notably in Arab countries, is by the device of paying an agent. Here a third party enters into the transaction. In itself this need not create a moral problem; we use estate agents to sell houses in Britain without having qualms about it. In certain countries, the services of an agent who knows the language, the relevant institutions and the government departments intimately is absolutely essential. The agent will also know what are the appropriate acts of hospitality to offer in order to cultivate close relationships. He performs a crucial function as middle-man, and there is nothing in principle wrong with paying him a percentage of the contract's values as a reward for services proffered.

However, a moral question still remains as to how the destiny of a contract is ultimately decided. Is part of the fee paid to the agent used to feather the nest of the relevant minister? Is paying an agent a 'special payment' at one remove, or something more akin to a 'customary payment'? The answer probably varies from agent to agent, and from country to country. It may be that in many cases a company prefers not to know; ask no questions and you get no lies. It is sufficient to say that the practice may in some circumstances be perfectly respectable, but it is riddled with ambiguity. It spares an organization direct responsibility for the decision of whether or not to bribe.

What help does the Bible provide on this whole subject? In the Old Testament the Hebrew word *shohadh* is variously translated 'gift' or 'bribe', depending on whether the context implies disapproval. In Proverbs 18.16, the effects of a gift are simply described: 'A man's gift makes room for him and brings him before great men.' But the usual context is one of condemnation:

> You shall take no bribe, for a bribe blinds the officials, and subverts the cause of those who are in the right.
> *Exodus 23.8*

> You shall not pervert justice; you shall not show partiality; and you shall not take a bribe, for a bribe blinds the eyes of the wise and subverts the cause of the righteous.
> *Deuteronomy 16.19*

> For I know how many are your transgressions, and how great are your sins –
> you who afflict the righteous, who take a bribe, and turn aside the needy in the gate.
> *Amos 5.12*

Most of the biblical references condemn bribery in the context of the law court. There, payments to officials are improper because they threaten the impartial administration of justice. They particularly imperil the position of the poor. The business situations under consideration in this chapter are not quite the same. Nevertheless, the biblical context of law may help us to ask the right sort of question about these modern-day dilemmas. What is just in this situation? Is the payment I am considering making a species of injustice? Does it have the effect of blinding the eyes, of obscuring the better judgement of those who hold positions of power and influence? Does it mean that tenders will be awarded by quite inappropriate criteria, which is not in the public interest? If the answers to these questions appear to be yes, such payments should not be offered.

Nevertheless, in general terms this is an area which precludes the luxury of easy answers. With regard to the different sort of payments discussed, there appears to be an ascending order of moral gravity, from gifts, through extortion, to outright bribes. There is a spectrum of acceptability at one end, to unacceptability at the other, with some greyer areas in between. There is also a distinction between demanding payments on the one hand, and acceding to demands on the other. It is more blameworthy to extort than to give in to extortion, though the latter course should be avoided as much as possible.

The problems do not only affect commercial organizations. Charities also face similar pressures. In order to get aid to the places which need it most, they may have to pay protection money to people posing as 'escorts'. This creates an especially acute dilemma: does the worthiness of the end (for example, feeding starving Somalian children) override the irregularity of the means, or does the contrast between means and end make such action more difficult to justify?[13]

Faced with moral problems of this complexity, the leader with integrity has a challenge. He or she needs to understand the dilemmas experienced by staff who are out in the field. People who confront the hard questions day by day have the right to know what the organization expects of them.

Certainly, individual companies need more specific guidance than that provided in the (British) Institute of Management's *Code of Conduct and Guides to Professional Management Practice*. Under section 4, the code says that the professional manager should 'neither offer nor accept any gift, favour or hospitality intended as, or having the effect of, bribery and corruption'.[14] However, under section

6 it says that the professional manager should, 'wherever practicable, comply with the professional standards set out in the Code of Conduct and Guides, but not necessarily be deemed to be in breach of obligations as a member of the Institute if complying with established overseas customs and practices which are inconsistent in detail with the foregoing.'[15] This certainly begs a few questions! It probably reflects the diversity of practice among British firms, and the difficulty there might have been in giving a more specific ruling to which managers in general could have given assent. But when it comes to individual organizations, a leader with integrity should not leave staff in a quandary as to whether the rules against bribery which apply at home do or do not apply when operating overseas.

Astuteness and Compromise

The issue of bribery is interesting and important in its own right, but I have used it principally as an example of the difficulties which can be involved in putting integrity into practice. If improper payments are not a problematical issue in your own area of work, I trust you can think of comparable issues which require a similar dexterity of moral judgement.

The fact is, of course, that organizations do not exist simply to act ethically. The better ones aspire to do so – some, like the Body Shop, even have strong ideological aims[16] – but their principal concerns are providing a service or making money.[17] Leaders cannot afford to be so bound up with questions of integrity that they take their eyes off the basic goals of the organization. One problem in looking at case studies in business ethics is that they abstract people from the pressures under which decisions are made, putting so sharp a focus on the problematical decision that they ignore the wider setting. In a computerized business ethics game which I have developed with a

friend from Newcastle Business School, we have sought to
address this problem by setting some typical moral dilemmas within the context of ongoing commercial decisions
about levels of production, pricing and investment.[18] Part-
icipants are trying to win on two counts, financial success
and moral integrity. Anything less would be unrealistic.

In the research on leadership qualities most appreciated
by employees, which I cited earlier, a second key characteristic alongside that of integrity was basic competence.[19]
People want leaders who are able to deliver. If they are
going to deliver, integrity by itself is not enough. Integrity
needs to be accompanied by *astuteness*.

The word 'astute' might sound less moral in tone. For
some it has the sinister connotation of 'crafty'; I see it
rather as 'shrewd'. Astuteness does not disparage or tone
down high-flown moral sentiment, but couches it in a
context of realism. Astute leaders rightly seek to turn
situations to their organization's financial advantage. In
doing so, they draw upon a variety of tactical skills. They
know when to bluff and when to cajole; how to out-think
and outpace the competition; when it is appropriate to play
cards close to one's chest in delicate negotiation; how far
to cut when decisive measures to save money have to be
made. But if astuteness is to be saved from plain sharp
practice,[20] it needs to be married to the qualities of integrity I have described earlier.

This leads me to a brief discussion of the place of
compromise. For many people 'compromise' is a rather
pejorative word. It suggests settling on a course of action
which is morally tainted: an abandonment of principle for
the sake of expediency. Clearly, there are many compromises which are nothing better than that, and therefore
deserving of criticism. But there is a much more positive
way of viewing compromise.

Some compromises are an attempt to do justice to
different moral claims, both or all of which are valid. The

mission statements I mentioned at the beginning of this chapter underline the fact that companies owe and generally acknowledge responsibilities to a range of different groups: shareholders, employees, customers, business partners, and the wider community.[21] Much of the time, there is no serious conflict between the interests and expectations felt by these different groups in relation to the company. Sometimes, especially when times are hard, there will be a clash. Faced with the necessity to cut costs, the company may have to choose between reducing the shareholders' dividend, making some staff redundant, narrowing the product range for its customers, delaying payment to its suppliers, or slowing down a process of cleaning up its act environmentally.

Often it will be appropriate to spread the burden of cost. Compromise then has the character of seeking to balance the interests, and maintain the confidence, of different groups, rather than completely abandoning one group in favour of another. But my main point is that sheer financial reality often constrains an organization so that it cannot meet the legitimate moral claims represented by these different groups as fully as it would like.

There are other compromises which are more clearly a case of making some concession to the *fallen* realities of this world, inside and outside organizations. To some extent, we are constrained by the forces and standards which operate in the world around us. We may reluctantly have to accept some things which are not satisfactory, which we would like to change, but where it is outside our power to do so. The world can be a very evil place. On the other hand, it is possible to over-exaggerate this.

Consider again the issue of improper payments. A strong moral presumption against bribery still exists in many parts of the world. Even in countries where it is widely practised, bribes are still not usually given or received openly, indicating a measure of shame and discomfiture

attached to the practice. But what lies behind this presumption, this reluctance to buy unfair advantage? In part,
it is an acknowledgment that one owes moral obligations
to one's *competitors*, a group of people who do not even get
a mention in most mission statements. Perhaps a reluctance
to pay bribes is the nearest the secular world gets to recognizing some truth in the Christian duty to love one's
enemy.

How should we understand compromise theologically?
We need to take seriously what Jesus says about the nature
of the kingdom of God, that it is present and future, now
and not yet, inaugurated but not consummated. The fact is
that Christians stand in a field of tension between two
ages; the present world which is one day to pass away, and
the coming world which will replace it and already makes
inroads upon it. Christians are called out of their old life
into a new existence, and yet they still have to live in a far
from perfect world with all the limitations on action
which that brings. They therefore stand in a relationship
both of continuity and discontinuity with the conventions
and practices of the present world.

If compromise is to be understood in this way, it is
important to affirm the element of tension. Where this is
lacking, compromise easily degenerates into uncritical conformity, a complacent acceptance of the *status quo*. The
best compromises are those which take the 'promise' part
of the word 'compromise' seriously. In other words, they
are creative, and hold out hope for something better in the
future.

Serpents and Doves

I come, finally, to the title of this chapter. When Jesus sent
out his disciples on a missionary journey, he did so with
this intriguing message: 'Behold I send you out as sheep in
the midst of wolves; so be wise as serpents and innocent

as doves' (Matthew 10.16). The danger wolves posed for sheep is obvious, but the juxtaposition of images in the second half of the saying makes a startling contrast. Why does Jesus associate serpents with wisdom? Probably because of Genesis 3.1: 'Now the serpent was more subtle than any other wild creature that the Lord God had made.' Why does he associate doves with innocence? Commentators are less sure about this, but possibly because doves are white, the symbol of purity. To be both serpent-like and dove-like seems a blatant contradiction, but this is the balance of attitudes Jesus commands of his disciples. He warns them both to be on their guard against persecution, and to be faithful and unsullied by evil in the face of it.

The relevance of these words of Jesus does not seem to me to be limited to first-century Christian missionaries. They have something to say about every Christian's vocation to live in the world. They are particularly telling for those called to be leaders. 'Wise as serpents, innocent as doves': they combine that mixture of idealism tempered by realism, principle laced with shrewdness, integrity married to astuteness, which are just the attitudes leaders need. Leaders help nobody by being naive, yet they also need to maintain a purity of thought, speech and action. It is indeed a testing vocation.

4

Thin Skin, Thick Skin

Managing the Dynamics of Change

'The reality of change is inescapable. If we do not change the inexorable forces of economics and shifts in the external world will force change upon us.'[1] So wrote John Harvey-Jones, former Chairman of ICI, in *Making It Happen*, the first of the stream of books he has written since his retirement in 1989. He was clearly right, and the truth of his words is being fully borne out by what is happening in the world around us in the mid-1990s.

In the sphere of business, the phenomenon of global competition, the awe-inspiring standards set by Japan, the rapid economic growth in other Far Eastern countries like South Korea, Taiwan and Malaysia, the economic transitions of Central and Eastern Europe, and the breakdown of cartels (official and unofficial), have all conspired to make the world market a very different place from what it was a generation ago. The ingenuity and pace of technological development are breathtaking. Until the early 1980s, computers were largely restricted to office desks, but now they accompany us everywhere, into our bedrooms and with us on our journeys. I have just read a paper on the future perspectives of information technology which says there should soon be no physical reason why one hand-held device should not incorporate all the features of a telephone, pager, electronic organizer, calculator, fax machine, and Nintendo games machine.[2] When that does come about, I am sure of one thing: that my ten-year-old son will master it quicker than me!

Change is a necessity in business, even for companies with a proven record of success. Success, about which I will say more in chapter five, can all too easily breed complacency. A good example of this is Lloyd's of London. Decade after decade of success left it ill-prepared for the series of catastrophes which occurred in the late 1980s and early 90s. The huge claims resulting from a series of unprecedented natural disasters, asbestos and pollution litigation in the United States, and dubious machinations within an under-regulated market, have led to personal bankruptcy and suicide on a horrifying scale. The risks which were always present in a system of unlimited liability have come home to roost for countless Names.[3]

Another example is the Swiss watch industry, which prided itself on its elegant watches made according to traditional mechanical design. The development of new electronic digital watches, spearheaded by companies from Japan, took the industry almost fatally by surprise.

Awareness of what the competition are or may be doing has in fact become one of the major catalysts for change. One company, for which a visit to Japan proved a salutary eye-opener, was Ford. In the mid-1970s, the British side of Ford's operations presented a curiously mixed picture. Ford cars were selling well, and the company appeared to hold sway in Britain's largely captive market. But this apparent state of well-being was deceptive. The management style was authoritarian, the union style militant. Efficiency levels were poor, and strikes, real or threatened, were a regular feature of the company's annual round of pay bargaining.

In 1978, Bill Hayden, Vice-President of Manufacturing for Ford of Europe, visited Japan to gauge for himself the nature and extent of the rumoured coming competition. The experience dealt him a severe shock. He realized that Japanese companies like Toyota and Nissan were years ahead of Ford in terms both of technology and the levels of commitment and co-operation they were able to conjure from the workforce. If Ford failed to change its production methods, keep abreast of the latest technology, and break its destructive mould of internecine strife, he believed that it was doomed. The company needed to discover a new competitive edge.

This visit proved a turning-point in Ford's history, so much so that Ford workers date their recent history in terms of 'Before' and 'After Japan' – the latter even being referred to as AJ! The message which Bill Hayden brought back was communicated effectively to the whole of the workforce. Gradually, over a period of years, things changed for the better in a big way.

All Change?

But change is also unpredictable. No one, least of all those who considered themselves experts on what was happening in Eastern Europe, predicted the rapid collapse of Communism during that dramatic year of 1989. With the end of the so-called Cold War, western armed forces were cut substantially and the defence industry found its future in doubt. It faced the challenge of diversifying in order to survive. But the ex-Communist countries are hardly enjoying a smooth transition to free-market, western-style democracies, and some remain very unstable. More information is now coming to light about the numbers of countries developing nuclear and chemical weapons systems. The defence industry could yet experience a call to expand again in response.

Sometimes there is a significant gap between the development of technology and ways being found for its effective use by human beings. To return to hand-held computers: watches incorporating calculators, organizers and pagers are already available, but at present only the most dedicated technophiles use them because they are just too awkward for most of us. There is a limit to how close together buttons can be packed, and it is unlikely that our fingers are going to grow any smaller! We have the challenge of making technology our servant and not our master.

In this rapidly changing world there is also the odd example of an organization which needs to change very little in order to continue being successful. Coca-Cola has marketed the same product in much the same packaging very successfully for the last 105 years. When it briefly changed its formula, in the mid-1980s, its major rival Pepsi-Cola seized on this as an admission of inadequacy; the public also preferred the original taste. So Coca-Cola reverted back very quickly. The development of Diet Coke can hardly be claimed as a major innovative shift.

A further word of caution is necessary about embracing an 'all change' philosophy too readily. Putting all its emphasis on new products and new processes, a company can end up in a confused situation, wasting people's energy and seeing nothing through to a proper conclusion. It is a mistake to try to change everything at once. Many people are by nature quite conservative, and they need reassuring signs of stability amidst the change.[4] Often an unwavering commitment to core values will serve both employees and customers in good stead during a radical reorganization in corporate affairs. If the company has built up a well-earned reputation for the care it demonstrates for its employees, or the speed with which it carries out repairs, it would be most unwise to jettison this for the sake of spurious short-term goals. Discernment is needed to distinguish change which is vital and necessary from change which is trivial and faddish.

Nevertheless, the basic picture is clear. In general terms, the premium on rapid change is very high. Nor does it only affect business. Schools have had to respond to a whole series of new government requirements, not least the National Curriculum. Behind these lay concerns about educational standards, fuelled by the dissatisfaction felt by many employers about the school-leavers in their workforce. Churches need to respond to the fact that their member- ship numbers, and with that their finances, are steadily dropping, quite apart from any other motive they may have for reaching people with the gospel. In virtually every area of life, there is a recognition that 'more of the same', an unchanged product in an unchanged package, will no longer satisfy. Things have to change. It is hardly surprising, then, that managing the dynamics of change has become a key requirement of successful leadership. Drawing upon Christian insights, allied with the best in management literature, I suggest five important aspects to managing change. They are: vision, communication, consultation, sensitivity and resilience.

Vision

First of all, a leader must decide what change is appropriate. What I have in mind here are not minor or incidental adjustments, but significant changes linked to the funda- mental direction in which the organization is heading. These changes should be consistent with the leader's over- all *vision* for the organization.

The need for a visionary element in leadership is being increasingly recognized. Warren Bennis has actually de- fined leadership as 'the capacity to create a compelling vision and translate it into action and sustain it.' He goes on to say that 'with a vision, the leader provides the all- important bridge from the present to the future of the organization.'[5]

Christians are fond of quoting Proverbs 29.18 in this context: 'Where there is no vision, the people perish.' In fact, this Authorised Version translation may not be the most accurate rendering of the verse; an alternative is:

'Where there is no prophecy, the people cast off restraint' (RSV). Whatever the precise meaning of the Hebrew, there seems to be a lot of truth in the familiar words of the Authorised Version. Most people like to have some picture of where it is they are heading. They struggle without vision; they look to their leaders to provide vision.

However, it has to be said that in today's rapidly changing world it is difficult to look very far ahead with any certainty. We also need to heed the warning in James 4.13-16 about being too presumptuous about what is going to happen. James reminds us that we are 'a mist that appears for a little time and then vanishes', and that the proper qualification to all our plans is 'if the Lord wills, we shall live and we shall do this or that'. But conditional on that basic humility and provisionality, there is nothing wrong in setting out what we hope and aspire to see happen. In many organizations, five or seven years will be the limit beyond which one cannot predict the future with any confidence. But the horizon will vary from one area of life and one business sector to another. The pharmaceuticals industry is an example of a sector which thinks in very long time-spans, because it can take as much as twelve to fifteen years to see a drug from the incipient idea, through the research and trial stages, to its selling on the pharmacist's shelf.

Ideally, the leader has a vision of people's lives transformed or significantly enhanced by the achievements of his or her organization. It is therefore vital that the leader believes that the core business of the organization is something intrinsically worthwhile. Only then can he or she inspire others.

Where do visions come from? Sometimes a vision may come directly from God. In the Bible, this is clearly the case. Abraham had a repeated vision that, despite the barrenness of his marriage, he would become the father of a great nation (Genesis 12.1-3; 15.1-6; 17.1-8). Ezekiel had strange ecstatic experiences which left him in no doubt that God was going to visit his people Israel in terrible judgement (Ezekiel 2–3; 11). Paul had a vision at Troas of a man beseeching him to 'come over to Macedonia and help us' (Acts 16.9). That provided the green light for Paul to begin his ministry in the provinces of Greece.

Sometimes biblical visions involve dreams and their interpretation. Joseph is an interesting example of this, because the interpretation he was given of Pharaoh's dreams enabled him to suggest sensible strategic planning for the years of famine in Egypt which he predicted would follow the years of plenty (Genesis 41). He faced up squarely to the reality of hard times coming, and so was able to manage a crisis several years before it became a crisis! An important point here, and one which is missing from modern business literature, is that visions are not uniformly optimistic. We cannot live in a period of economic growth all the time, and sometimes the visionary leader is one who sees hard times coming and takes the necessary action, well in advance, to avert the worst consequences of them.

Biblical visions are therefore God-given. The New Testament depicts them as characteristic of life under the new covenant. Peter cites Joel chapter 2 on the Day of Pentecost:

> And on the last days it shall be, God declares,
> that I will pour out my Spirit upon all flesh,
> and your sons and your daughters shall prophesy,
> and your young men shall see visions,
> and your old men shall dream dreams.
> Acts 2.17

I have come across people receiving visions in the context of church life. I have also come across this phenomenon with regard to personal circumstances, such as whom one is going to marry. What is rarer, but far from unknown, is people having visions which they feel are directly God-given in relation to their secular work. Clearly, great care is needed here in assuring non-Christian members in an organization that one is not simply following irrational whims or harbouring delusions of grandeur. A vision needs to be spelt out in terms that are acceptable across the barriers of religion and race.

In a working context, I suggest that visions are much more likely to be the result of solid, painstaking analysis, though one should not be closed to the intuitive element which operates more in terms of 'hunches' about what is going to happen. A managing director in the furnishings industry whom I interviewed spoke of the importance of *thinking things through* very carefully before starting on a new course of action. For his company this resulted in an avowed aim not simply to serve the customer but to *delight* the customer. This led to a policy of developing innovative products, rather than defending market share with existing products, which was the prevailing mindset in his business sector. By a far-sighted, thoughtful approach, he was stealing a march on his competitors.

Christian leaders of organizations will not normally bypass this process of careful reflection. They need to take realistic stock of the present situation, arming themselves with as much relevant information as possible. Leaders must beware of thinking they know this automatically. I recall one of our theological students at Ridley Hall going on a parish placement. The vicar assured him that this was a parish which consisted largely of elderly people. Even a cursory sociological survey by the student revealed that this was not the case. The number of elderly people living in the area was no more than average, but the vicar had been swayed into thinking otherwise by the preponderance of elderly people in his congregation, and the fact that he directed his pastoral ministry mainly towards such people.

Sometimes a new investigation of the facts produces striking and revealing results.

I know of one ailing company where there was a per-
ceived problem on the sale side. But it wasn't until a new,
locum managing director came in that it was discovered
that two of the four salespeople were procuring 85 per
cent of the sales; the other two were contributing almost
nothing to the sales effort.

Good leaders glean information and welcome opinions
from a variety of sources. To understand their organization
better, they talk to a wide cross-section of people – a diag-
onal slice – across it. To prevent being trapped in their
own particular sector's way of looking at things, they keep
their eyes and ears open for significant trends and emerging
good practice in other sectors as well. They live in a state
of constant mental alertness. They are astute observers.

I believe this was true of Old Testament prophets like
Isaiah, Jeremiah and Amos. It was not only that they were
open to receive the word of God, crucial though that was.
It was more a case of God adding a supernatural dimension
to well-developed natural capacities. The prophets were
astute observers of what was happening on the national
and international scene, seeing behind external religious
observance to moral and spiritual realities, discerning
God's hand in the rise and fall of nations. A graphic
example of this is found in Isaiah 45. Cyrus, the Persian
king whose defeat of Babylon led to the end of the Jewish
exile, is described as 'the Lord's anointed': one who is
called by name even 'though you do not know me' (Isaiah
45.6). The prophet had observed what was happening in
Middle Eastern politics and put two and two together in a
discerning way.

In chapter two, I pointed to three key New Testament
images which are used about leaders: servant, shepherd
and steward. Even though the Bible uses these mainly in
a church context, I suggested that they all have something

significant to say about leadership in a secular context as well. I would now like to add a fourth: the Greek word *episkopos*, which is usually translated 'bishop', but which literally means 'overseer': someone who watches over. To maintain my series of alliterative words, I am tempted to use the word 'supervisor', but I think overseer conveys the sense better. A good leader exercises oversight. To do that, he or she needs to have a good overall picture. Whereas others (presumably many of the managers under him or her) have a more detailed knowledge of particular parts of the picture, the leader sees how the particular fits into the general, providing an understanding which is more complete. The leader has a very important watching brief.

Performing this watching brief well is what equips leaders for the formulation of visions. But we must beware of conceiving this in too individual a manner. Leadership is usually exercised in a collective way. There will not normally be a single individual who exercises the role of overseer alone. A substantial number of people may play a part in developing a vision, and it is important – at the innovative stage – that people be encouraged to share ideas freely.

At ICI's Millbank headquarters, John Harvey-Jones deliberately removed strategic planning meetings from the imposing splendour of the board room, to a room which was much more informally arranged. He writes: 'I wanted our executive team to operate as a band of brothers, where discussion was free and uninhibited, where people could get up and walk around, pour themselves a cup of coffee, argue, draw things on flip charts, gesticulate, and generally feel free and unrestricted.'[6] It is this sort of atmosphere which is conductive to the generation of vision.

The key insight, idea or image in a vision may in fact originate from anywhere. The person in the most senior position of leadership should not be proudly possessive, feeling that it has to come from him. But once the idea has been adopted, once the vision has taken shape, it is vital that the leader thoroughly owns it. The leader has the responsibility of enthusing others with the vision, and of keeping it 'bright and shining'.[7]

For the Christian leader there is an extra dimension, though it may be one of which she hesitates to speak in a secular context. That is, a confidence, when facing the future, in the infinite possibilities of God. When Nehemiah, a Jewish exile living in Persia, heard that the city of Jerusalem was virtually a ruin, his first reaction was one of abject despair; but as he mourned and pondered so there developed a vision of a rebuilt wall and a restored city. Probably in fear and trembling, but with a fervent prayer to 'the God of heaven' (Nehemiah 2.4) he presented his concern to King Artaxerxes, who showed both sympathetic understanding and an unexpected willingness to facilitate Nehemiah's project (Nehemiah 2.8–9). In time, Nehemiah duly put his vision into effect, though not without having to face much discouragement and a concerted attempt by those arch-schemers, Sanballat and Tobiah, to undermine the rebuilding. Upon its completion, the surrounding nations were forced to acknowledge that 'this work had been accomplished with the help of our God' (Nehemiah 6.16).

Communication

Second, a leader has to communicate the vision. It is clearly no use if the vision remains his or her possession alone. The vision, and the strategy which follows from it, must be communicated clearly and memorably to others in the organization.

Visions can often be crystallized in terms of a simple image or a catchy phrase. Steve Jobs, the founder of Apple, coined the phrase 'one person, one computer' to express his vision of a society in which everyone was able to make use of a highly-powered informational tool. The slogan which Ford repeatedly use on their adverts, 'everything we do is driven by you', conveys a neat *double entendre* of receptivity to customer desires and success in satisfying them. In the business world, the coining of a new logo can be a psychologically important way of indicating a significant change in direction. A few years ago, Prudential swopped the 'man from the Pru' image for a Prudence symbol, which they thought better reflected its diverse range of activities and modern commercial approach.

Examples can also be given from other spheres of life. Graham Cray, the Principal of Ridley Hall, has recently given students a more secure grasp of the college's evangelical identity by speaking (repeatedly) of 'roots down, walls down'. By this he means roots firmly down in the evangelical tradition, and being unapologetic about that, but 'walls down' in the sense of dismantling barriers which prevent us from being open to positive aspects in other Christian traditions. What more vivid crystallization of future hope could there be than the image Moses used of the promised land, 'a land flowing with milk and honey' (Deuteronomy 6.3)? For Paul, the 'body of Christ' (1 Corinthians 12.27) was a rich expression which conveyed both the close identity he felt Christian believers had with the risen Christ, and their interdependence as members of the church. We must not underestimate the power of a key idea, memorably expressed.

For leaders, the importance of crisp, clear communication extends beyond the sharing of a vision. It relates to much more detailed matters as well. Few things cause more grumbles in organizations than 'being kept in the dark', 'not knowing what is going on', 'being given conflicting pieces of information'. I know an educational institution where the letters which parents regularly received from the head were at one time a serious embarrassment. The poverty of the syntax obscured the sense; the failure to check facts rendered the information unreliable. Leaders engender much more confidence if they are skilled communicators. This does not necessarily mean they have to be fine public orators. There are many different ways of communicating in the modern world. Effectiveness is what counts, not aesthetics.

Consultation

On the whole, people respond positively to visions. They are uplifted, encouraged or stimulated by them. Even if their attitude is more cynical, the reaction is unlikely to be one of actual hostility. A vision is usually sufficiently long-term, sufficiently broad, that it poses no immediate threat. It is when the strategy of implementing the vision is translated into specific, substantial changes that attitudes are likely to become more mixed.

The sort of changes that are likely to disturb people are as follows: relocating a sphere of operations; taking out a level of management; introducing new technology which makes human labour redundant; rewriting the rule-book; expecting people to absorb additional responsibilities with no equivalent compensation. There may be excellent reasons for doing all of these things, but in each case there is a human cost. People need to be wooed carefully and sensitively if the operation is to be carried through with co-operation and goodwill.

This raises the question of what level of consultation is appropriate before a major change is launched. There is no simple right answer to this question. Sometimes the suddenness and severity of a crisis may render urgent changes necessary with a minimum of consultation. It is clear what needs to be done to avert disaster and prevent the ship from sinking; the luxury of time spent in consultative meetings simply cannot be afforded. However, such circumstances are unusual. Consultation is nearly always a must in order to show people respect, keep morale and confidence high, and glean good ideas about how change can be carried out smoothly and effectively. Rosabeth Moss Kanter, author of one of the most valuable business books on the subject, *The Change Masters* believes that masters of change are masters in 'participating' others.[8] The effects of not consulting people can be very damaging indeed.

I once interviewed the director of a charity who had presided over a major organizational change two years previously. The change concerned an attempt to unify the social and fundraising sides of the work, by giving these two aspects of the charity's work common regional boundaries – a feature they had previously lacked. This seemed to make obvious sense to the higher echelons of management in the charity. But they failed to consult more widely, with the result that when the change was announced, it was met first with a stunned and then an angry reaction from both social workers and fundraisers. Their resentment was not so much about the change *per se*, as the fact that they had not been consulted. For two months, the organization was, in the words of the director, 'totally unmanageable'.

A contrasting tale was told to me by someone who has held a number of senior positions in the food industry. In the late 1970s, he was UK Operations Director for an American multinational which owned a number of businesses in this country. One was located in South Yorkshire, near Sheffield; it had been operating for seven years and consistently ran at a loss. The other was located in Brighton; it had been running for 107 years and was profitable. The multinational had already made a provisional decision to close the Yorkshire factory. My friend spent a sleepless night pondering the situation and came to the conclusion that this was mistaken: Sheffield should stay open and Brighton should close. The Brighton operation should move to Sheffield. This might seem perverse, but his reasoning was twofold. First, the Yorkshire plant was modern and purpose-built, whereas the Brighton plant was antiquated. Second, as the economy stood at that time, he considered the social cost of a major lay-off would be far greater in South Yorkshire than in Sussex. Workers from the Brighton plant could find new employment more easily.

For all the logic of his case, he anticipated considerable resistance to his plan. There is a natural reaction of 'that's unfair!' when a group of workers who produce a profitable product make way for another group who make an unprofitable one. But the Operations Director pushed the change through with remarkable ease. He discussed the proposal with workers' representatives, and succeeded in convincing them that the move made sense, before going back to the parent company and asking them to change their mind. By being absolutely honest, putting the case persuasively, and treating people with respect, he enlisted the workers' co-operation in a smooth and straightforward transition. Four Brighton employees migrated north to the redeveloped factory in Yorkshire; most of the remainder found alternative employment. The relocation cost about £1 million, but in the next eighteen months the subsidiary company's market share almost doubled.

The nature and extent of consultation depends on many factors, such as the size of the organization, how effective and well respected the structures of representation are within it, and what type of organization it is. I shall return to this last point shortly.

What consultation almost invariably reveals, of course, is that not everyone is supportive of a proposed change. Leaders are often faced by a workforce which wants to change less quickly or drastically than he or she deems necessary. A crucial question therefore consists in knowing what degree of support is needed before one goes ahead with the change. Researchers indicate that with respect to most proposals for change, a number of different groups can be identified:

- **innovators** – enthusiasts for change in general
- **early adopters** – people of more measured judgement who are willing to give change a chance if a strong case can be made for it
- **late adopters** – cautious people who need more convincing, either by the precedent of early adopters, or hard evidence of the proposed change working elsewhere
- **laggards** – people with a strong antipathy to change

One might also add:

- **resisters** – people who do not merely drag their feet, but may actually try to sabotage the process of change

If a leader is faced with such a spectrum of responses, but remains convinced of the desirability and necessity of the proposed change, how should he or she proceed? How long should one persevere in the attempt to persuade all and sundry?

John Finney, Bishop of Pontefract and formerly the Church of England's officer spearheading the Decade of Evangelism, has some wise words on this in his book, *Understanding Leadership*.[9] He says that it is no good delaying change until everyone has come to a common mind. Endless consultation rarely produces uniformity, and in the meantime, enthusiasts for change become frustrated. The right moment probably lies when the leaders have won the support of the innovators and early adopters, and are just beginning to encroach upon the crucial (and probably most numerous) body of late adopters. If the decision is then made to go ahead with change, many of these late adopters, acceding to a sense of the inevitable, will probably fall in and start pulling their weight. I suspect that in many cases, the laggards will come along screaming and shouting in due course, while the active resisters, should they persist, may need to be offered the possibility of an exit route.

Finney's book is an attempt to apply modern management thinking to the world of the church. His analysis of the most appropriate timing for change is made with that context in mind. In a commercial organization, time may be at a greater premium, and decisions may have to be made more quickly, leaving a shorter period for consultation. Charities and voluntary organizations typically proceed more slowly because they cannot afford to alienate too many of their supporters. That is one reason why the pace of change in church life tends to be slow. Those who do not like a change vote with their feet. In a company setting, they are more likely to stomach change and live with it.

Nevertheless, enlisting people's goodwill, and seeking to spark a mood of enthusiasm about change, remain desirable in any setting. In persuading people of the necessity for change, there are usually two important factors to play on: one negative and one positive. The negative factor is discontent with how things are at present – usually expressed as: 'we really can't carry on as we are'. When you sit down openly with people and get them to face facts squarely, they will often admit this is the case. The positive factor is the vision of how things could be in the future – the carrot of something far, far better. Those who are enthusiasts for change – the people whom Kanter calls 'prime movers' or 'ideas champions' – need to be encouraged to spread this vision as widely as possible.

Sensitivity

Even where people are convinced of the need for change on an intellectual level, there are still obstacles which have to be taken seriously at an emotional level. A further challenge of leadership is therefore to be sensitive to people's feelings. I once visited a company where the leadership had decided to split the operation between two sites, and along different lines to the existing structure: along market divisions rather than product divisions. This was a wise strategic move, which made eminent business sense, but it had upset many employees because it meant they were no longer working alongside colleagues who had become close friends.

Good leaders are sympathetic to such considerations; they understand the pain involved and show they understand by talking directly with the people who are hurt. They may be willing to make marginal adjustments to the strategy to reduce the pain and ease the transition. It may also be appropriate to give people freedom for expressions of nostalgia and grief about the past – to be sad about what they are losing. When a corporate unit closes down, there needs to be some significant social event to mark the occasion. Tears should be allowed to flow, as well as glasses to be filled, on that final organizational visit to the local pub. I have even heard of an industrial chaplain holding the equivalent of a funeral service to mark a plant closure. Not everybody turned out, but a substantial proportion of the workforce did.

The need for sensitivity to people's feelings points to an even deeper quality in a leader. It points to the fact that a leader must love the people he or she leads. This might sound rather embarrassing, sentimental language in a business context, but I think the Christian should be prepared to speak of love where others might employ the rather cooler term 'care'. The nearest that modern management jargon comes to employing the word 'love', curiously, is in the cryptic context of the much-used acronym TLC – Tender Loving Care! However, I have heard of one tough-minded manager in the British car industry who once surprised a team, who had successfully seen a difficult project through to its conclusion, by breaking down in tears and saying that he loved them.

While some people are embarrassed by such open displays of emotion, many do respond, and a leader is likely to win commitment and loyalty rather than lose it by being unafraid to display personal warmth and affection. In the Old Testament, David was clearly a leader of this type. He was a man who wore his heart on his sleeve, and who inspired tremendous loyalty among his followers, both as a fugitive and as a king. A vivid example of this is the story of the three mighty men who risked their lives to fetch him a drink of water from the well of Bethlehem (2 Samuel 23.13–17). David was so overcome with emotion that he poured out the drink to the Lord, with the words: 'Shall I drink the blood of the men who went at the risk of their lives?'

However, true love goes much deeper than an overt show of emotion. On the whole, Jesus appears to have been less demonstrative in his emotions than David. Indeed, the New Testament theologian A. E. Harvey has suggested that the Gospel records of Jesus' life and teaching give few examples of action that was self-evidently loving. In his book *Strenuous Commands*, he argues that the New Testament 'inspiration for our loving is not the moral example afforded by Jesus in his life, but the theological imperative provided by his death.'[11] I have to say that I find this a rather superficial reading of the Gospels. There is much to be learnt from the sort of love Jesus showed, both as a leader of his disciples and in his encounters with others.

First, it is clear to my mind that Jesus displays empathy: a sympathetic understanding of what is going on inside people. For instance, he immediately grasps the social isolation and genuine searching of the crooked tax collector Zacchaeus. He takes a bold initiative in inviting himself to the little man's house for lunch, and secures a reformation in his business practice without the need for any further words said (Luke 19.1–10). With another rich man, the young ruler who aspired after eternal life, he was apparently less successful, but he shows both deep affection and cutting perception as he issues the challenge the man found too hard to accept: 'And Jesus looking upon him loved him, and said to him, "You lack one thing; go, sell what you have, and give to the poor, and you will have treasure in heaven; and come, follow me"' (Mark 10.21).

In another episode, James and John, two of Jesus' closest followers, could easily have driven him to distraction. Immediately after Jesus predicts the circumstances of his death, they approach him to ask for the best seats in the Kingdom to come. But Jesus responds with great patience, making it clear that those who sit with him in his glory must first be prepared to experience the dregs of his suffering (Mark 10.35–40; Luke 22.28–30). When Jesus shrewdly throws the disciples in at the deep end and sends them out on a mission, they come back exhilarated about what has happened: 'Lord, even the demons are subject to us in your name!' Jesus' response is to celebrate joyfully with them (Luke 10.1–24). His prayer of thanks for the special revelation God has given to the disciples must have been a great encouragement to them. There is in fact plenty of evidence in Jesus of that sympathetic understanding of what is going on inside people, which is so important for leaders nursing people through the process of change.

Another way in which Jesus demonstrates love is in his accessibility. This does not mean that he was necessarily a natural extrovert. Clearly, he liked to withdraw from public from time to time, treasuring the opportunity to be on his own with God in prayer (Mark 1.35). But the interest his actions had stirred up made this difficult. On two occasions in Mark's Gospel, we read of Jesus trying to get away from the crowds, but then abandoning this plan of action when he was confronted by the needs of the desperate people who pursued him. In the first case, it was the Galilean crowd, whom he saw as 'sheep without a shepherd' (Mark 6.31–34); and in the second, it was the woman from Syrian Phoenicia with the sick daughter (Mark 7.24–30). Jesus' receptivity to people at their point of need made it difficult for him to say no.

The Gospels include numerous vignettes of Jesus interacting with other people, whether as individuals or in groups. What is striking is the fullness of attention he gives to each person. Even when he is in a hurry to meet one engagement, he is prepared to break off to attend to someone in an obvious state of need. Consider his compassionate treatment of the woman with the blood condition who touched him en route to the sickbed of Jairus's daughter (Mark 5.21–34).

There is a lesson here for busy leaders who feel that they are forever being sidetracked by unexpected requests. It is tempting to retreat behind a desk or a secretary and make ourselves inaccessible to the world outside the office, especially when we have a long list of tasks that we desperately want to get done today. Of course, this is a measure we may have to resort to occasionally in order to clear major backlogs of work. But the main quality we need to cultivate is one of accessibility. A leader is in the business of handling people, and people need to know that he or she is ready and available to oil troubled relationships, discuss technical problems, and firefight unforeseen emergencies – or else that these tasks are properly delegated. Such difficulties are especially apt to arise when an organization is going through a period of substantial change. If employees can never get through to their leader, or they sense that his or her mind is half elsewhere when they do, they will soon stop trying – with potentially disastrous consequences for staff cohesion and morale.

One of the differences between managers and leaders highlighted by Craig Hickman, whom I cited in chapter two, is that between Management by Objectives (MBO) and Management by Walking – or Wandering – Around (MBWA). The latter might seem casual to the point of being bizarre, but it has been practised very deliberately by one successful multinational company I have visited, Hewlett-Packard. Throughout its history, Hewlett-Packard has enjoyed an excellent track record in employee relations. A key factor in this is the emphasis placed on leaders' accessibility. The layout of Hewlett-Packard's factories is open plan, and a good deal of important discussion therefore takes place in hallways, by the coffee machine and over lunch. Alongside the stress on wandering around, runs what is known as an 'open door policy'. Staff are assured that no adverse consequences will result from responsibly raising issues with management or personnel. Managers' doors should be considered open for encouraging feedback, sharing feelings and frustrations, and putting forward proposals for improving ways of doing things. The ease of cummunication which results is a key component in successfully managing the dynamics of change.

Resilience

However well the process is handled, no leader managing the process of change can expect an easy ride. If she does get one, it should be treated as an unexpected bonus. Because change is so disruptive, because it usually creates losers as well as gainers, and because the benefits claimed for it may take time to come through, a certain amount of unpopularity is to be expected. Pioneers of change provoke resentment and receive flak. They need to have the strength of character to absorb it.

One business leader whom I much respect said: 'People need to be able to see the steel in you.' By nature he is an easy-going, laid-back sort of character. He is therefore liable to be underestimated. But behind the amiable exterior there is a man of steel, who knows his own mind and will face conflict fearlessly if necessary. A good leader is always willing to listen to reason, but he knows when people are wasting his time. He is firm, without being obstinate.

This brings us to another side of Jesus' character. There was a tough side to Jesus, which may or may not contribute to Harvey's difficulty in describing him as loving. I am thinking particularly of Jesus' capacity to challenge people. He knew that there was a time to rebuke as well as a time to build up. In the Gospels, there are times when Jesus does not spare the disciples some sharp words. He openly expresses his disappointment when they prove unequal to the task of coping with the boy suffering from a distressing fit (Mark 9.19). Simon Peter experiences in quick succession the joy of being called blessed (when he receives the insight that Jesus is the Christ), and the horror of being called Satan (when he thinks he knows better than Jesus what the destiny of this Christ will be – see Matthew 16.13–23). There are times when Jesus' handling of people might actually strike us as a bit harsh. We might wish that he was a little more the 'gentle Jesus, meek and mild', whom we were taught about at Sunday school. But Jesus' plain speaking had the best interests of individuals at heart. The capacity to challenge is not incompatible with a disposition of love; in fact, it is an essential component of it.

The lessons for organizational practice are clear to be seen. Love for those under the leader's authority is not to be confused with sentimentality. Love is a disposition which delights in other people and wills the best for them. Willing the best includes willing that they give of their best. A leader is therefore right to stretch staff and to expect work of high quality. When an individual or group are letting the company down, they need to be told so. When clear and unambiguous targets have been set, it is important to be rigorous about holding people to them.

The leader therefore has to hold together two contrasting characteristics in one person: *sensitivity* and *resilience*.

If leaders are convinced of the necessity of fundamental change, and they have the basic level of support they need, they will not be deterred by the opposition which comes their way. They will absorb the flak, redouble their efforts to persuade staff of the necessity of change, and persist until the benefits of change become evident. In managing the dynamics of change, leaders therefore need both sensitivity and resilience; to explain the title of this chapter, a combination of thin skin and thick skin! This is far easier said than done. It means on the one hand caring deeply about the unhappiness which is coming the way of others, and relatively little about the unpleasantness which is coming one's own way. Most of us, most of the time, are far more sensitive to our own pain than that of others. A leader who is managing change has to reverse this very natural tendency.

I end this chapter with a further reference to the Bible. The New Testament contains an interesting example of managing change, the more so because we have two different perspectives on it – those of the historian Luke, and of the apostle Paul, himself a major initiator of change. This is the process by which the early Christian church gradually developed from a minority Jewish grouping, and came to accept Gentile believers on an equal status with Jewish ones. As a Bible study project, I recommend reading the book of Acts and the epistles of Paul with the handling of this process as the principal subject in view.

Despite the command given by Jesus at the end of Matthew – 'Go therefore and make disciples of all nations . . .' – the universal scope of the gospel took time for the early church to fully comprehend and think through. The transition was far from straightforward. It was a process in which there were clear differences of emphasis between the various leaders, James, Peter and Paul, though Luke presents the three as standing together to propose an agreed way forward at the Council of Jerusalem in Acts 15.

Nevertheless, Luke's account reveals that acceptance of the Gentile Christians nearly foundered on the practical question: should they be required to be circumcised? Here Paul fought a hard battle to convince the Jewish Christians that the Gentiles did not need to be. In his letter to the Galatians, he has some hard things to say about the 'Judaisers', the Jewish Christians based in Jerusalem who were insisting on circumcision for Gentile converts. He hints that there may have been a considerable gulf between himself and the other apostles, and speaks of opposing Peter to his face, because on visiting Antioch he drew back from eating with the Gentile converts, 'fearing the circumcision party' (Galatians 2.12).

It is clear that on the issue of circumcision, Paul was absolutely uncompromising when he saw a basic theological principle at stake, as was the situation he describes in Galatians. Here we see the resilience of the man through and through. Nothing must be allowed to obscure the truth that Gentiles and Jews alike are justified by faith in Christ. But Paul could also be surprisingly flexible when he felt this basic theological principle was *not* at stake. So we read of his circumcising Timothy in Acts 16.1–3,[12] and of his readiness to mollify Jewish Christian sensitivities in Acts 21.17–26. There are times when he seeks to emphasize Christianity's continuity with Judaism, as well as times when he stresses its new departures.

Paul also had a fundamental concern that the early church should not be split into two halves, a Jewish half and a Gentile half, which had little to do with each other. In this respect his concern to collect money from the churches in Greece and Asia Minor for the impoverished church in Jerusalem is especially significant. Paul did not let his theological differences with the Jerusalem church stand in the way of practical financial concern for them.

In 2 Corinthians 8 and 9 we see him using a whole plethora of different arguments to persuade a church with no personal contact with the Jerusalem church to give generously for their relief: the impressive example of the Macedonian Christians (8.1–5); a certain amount of flattery (8.7); 'the grace of our Lord Jesus Christ, that though he was rich, yet for your sake he became poor' (8.9); the incentive to finish what they had started (8.10–11); the target of an equal distribution of resources (8.13–14); and so on. The variety of arguments used speaks volumes about the determination he had that, one way or another, the needed money should be raised.

What we see, then, is that Paul combined a toughness in dealing with the opponents of change with a fundamental compassion. He did not try to break his links with these opponents or wash his hands of them. Just as Jesus combined the characteristics of sensitivity and resilience in his own person, so did Paul. Modern business writers like Harvey-Jones, Bennis and Kanter may have much to teach us about handling the process of change, but there are also many valuable lessons to be learnt from the pages of scripture.

5

More Than Conquerors
Learning from Failure as Well as Success

'There's little that is more important to tomorrow's managers than failure. We need lots more of it. We need faster failure. It is fair to say that if we can't increase the gross national failure rate, we're in for a very rough ride indeed.' So writes Tom Peters in his international bestseller, *Thriving on Chaos*.[1] He exhorts companies to 'revel in thoughtful failures that result from fast action-taking',[2] and suggests that they publicly applaud and reward people who make interesting mistakes. Tom Peters is a guru who loves to shock and surprise!

There are Christian writers too who make much of failure. In her book *Gateway to Hope*, Maria Boulding characterizes Jesus as 'history's greatest failure'.[3] She complements John 1.14, 'the Word was made flesh and lived among us', with the sentence, 'the Word was made failure and died among us'.[4] She thinks that this is of enormous comfort to all who feel that they have failed: 'God has dealt with our failure by himself becoming a failure in Jesus Christ and so healing it from the inside.'[5] When Jesus died on the cross, it is of course true that he was scorned by his enemies, deserted by his friends, and apparently cursed by God. What more poignant picture of failure could there be?

If failure shows signs of becoming fashionable, success is becoming increasingly suspect. Many are reacting against a society which seems unhealthily success-oriented. Working on the money markets can give young people an enormous kick, and undreamt-of wealth – but is it really worth it if the work engenders a spirit of willingness to do anything in order to win, and a state of being burnt out by the age of thirty? Some Christians regard success as a synonym for worldliness, and point out that it is a word rarely found in the Bible. God's word of assurance to Joshua as he approached the invasion of the Promised Land (' . . . and then you shall have good success', in Joshua 1.8) is a very isolated occurrence. Success is a concept which has only attained its current importance in western society quite recently. It is an idol which needs tearing down from its throne.

Although I think there is a grain of truth in this analysis, and that failure can be a very instructive experience, I do not altogether agree with the views cited thus far. Tom Peters is far too flippant about failure. Failures are costly and painful. Jesus can ultimately be considered a failure only if the crucifixion is seen as the end of the story. It was not. (This is not, of course, to deny that Jesus' rejection at the hands of his own people contained an enormous element of tragedy.) The desire to succeed is, I believe, a basic and healthy aspect of our human nature. To call failure success, and success failure, renders our longings, goals and aspirations meaningless. There are certainly paradoxes to be found in this area, but they should not be pursued to the point of perversity. Who in practice enjoys failing and hates succeeding?

Taking Pleasure in Success

I will begin by affirming that there is nothing wrong in taking pleasure in success. Success can be defined and measured in a number of different ways which are not necessarily mutually exclusive. Let us consider three.

First, there is the successful *attainment of certain goals or targets*. As chairman of ICI, John Harvey-Jones set out the target of a £1000 million profit for the year 1984. It seemed a demanding target at the time, but it was reached. A research scientist longs to see the development and marketing of his product, an author the publication of her book, an architect the putting into effect of his design plans. When any such things are achieved, there is cause for satisfaction. Curiously, this is a pleasure which often passes us by – especially in the case of busy people like leaders. We pass on so quickly to our next target, we push last week's events so summarily to the back of our minds in our earnest absorption with this week's diary, that success goes unnoticed and unheralded.

I think we need to remember what God did when he had finished creating the world. He 'saw everything that he made, and behold, it was very good' (Genesis 1:31). On the seventh day, he rested from all the work which he had done. He contemplated his creation, and doubtless took satisfaction in it, a good job brought to a successful completion. I know the managing director of a ceramics firm who seeks to apply this principle in his own work. In a fascinating article on theology and work, he has written this:

The big moment for the development engineer is after the months of building to stand back, take a deep breath and press the green button. If it works (or rather, when it eventually works), it will of course be allowed to run for several minutes, whereas a few seconds were all that was strictly necessary. Those minutes of Sabbath rejoicing are not a luxury – they are an essential part of the creative process. There are many more examples of the Sabbath principle already in unconscious use in industry, and they should be recognised and encouraged. Farmers leaning over the gate chewing over the situation, salesmen opening the champagne to celebrate a large order, athletes releasing the tension by punching the air: all these complete the process, and bring the peace and contentment which is God's gift of the Sabbath. There is a tendency to come home and slump in front of the television, or go out and bash away in the shed, but one should consider whether it it not better just to sit down and reflect quietly over the day. A manager may want to forget about work, but maybe the work needs completion by "five minutes peace."[6]

Second, success can be understood not in relation to task but *in relation to person*. For many people, this will mean achieving a prestigious position, possessing a luxurious home, or earning a handsome salary. Christians should not delude themselves into thinking such things are automatically of no consequence to them. But hopefully their understanding of personal success goes deeper than this. At the end of a seminar we ran at Ridley Hall on 'Success and Failure in Business', one participant said he had come to see success in these terms: 'achieving my God-given potential in accordance with God's plan'. He was clearly on to something important here. We all have God-given gifts, and we have a responsibility to nurture and develop them. Perhaps we sometimes read Jesus' parable of the talents and wonder which of the servants we are most like: the one with ten talents, five or only one? The important thing, though, is not the number of talents we end up with, but whether we make the most of what we have been given.

In his latest book, *The Empty Raincoat*, Charles Handy tells the story of a rabbi called Zuzya of Hannipol. He spent his life lamenting his lack of talent and his failure to be another Moses. One day God said to him, 'In the coming world we will not ask you why you were not Moses, but why you were not Zuzya.'[7] It is no good imagining that we can ever be a carbon-copy of anyone else. God does not want us to be. He has made us all unique, and he wants us to express that uniqueness.

Leaders are likely to be particularly concerned with developing their gifts. The exercise of leadership makes tremendous demands. It requires a subtle mixture of very special qualities. No leader can pretend to have all of them; every leader, however impressive, has scope for improvement. If a person can look back at the end of his career and see how his leadership style improved, how his strengths were harnessed and his weaknesses contained, and how he handled comparable situations much better the second time around, then he has cause for satisfaction.

It is part of the very nature of the task, however, that leaders should not simply be concerned about the development of their own potential. They should be even more concerned about the development of other people's potential. For the sake of the individuals concerned and for the sake of the organization, they want to see those gifts blossom and grow.

I have a friend who is richly talented in many different areas. In everything he does he aspires to excel. What makes me sad is that when others excel, his competitive streak always leads him to compare their abilities with his own. Instead of simply enjoying another person's magnificent painting (he is an artist in his spare time), he finds it depressing because his one painting is not as good. How much better to rejoice and marvel at somebody else's skill, which does not have to be duplicated by oneself! Christian leaders should count among those who take pleasure in others' success.

Again, the leader's satisfaction will not simply be in the aggregate of others' achievements, individually assessed. She will rejoice in the harnessing and dovetailing of individual talents in a well-knit team. She will be pleased when people communicate honestly with each other, warmly encourage each other, and allow their own creative inputs to be transformed into a team effort which adds to their value.[8] Such a team effort is better than the sum total of the individual parts. The unity of fellowship which comes through a whole-hearted dedication to a common task is not something which is generated very easily. A leader who has the privilege of experiencing it, and who probably had some responsibility in evoking it, does indeed have something to smile about.

A third definition sees success as *performing a balancing act*. In previous chapters, I suggested qualities which leaders need to hold in an appropriate balance. We looked at the balance between . . .

- **Leadership and management** – the balance between directing and inspiring (the quintessential characteristics of leadership) and the more mundane but necessary activities of planning, organizing, controlling and evaluating – the fundamentals of management.
- **Servant and shepherd** – the self-effacing role of the servant, and the protective role of the shepherd.
- **Delegation and non-delegation** – delegating certain types of responsibility, but not delegating those which properly belong to a leader.
- **Astuteness and integrity** – astuteness in resolutely seeking corporate objectives, and integrity in the way one pursues them.
- **Moral standards and realism** – seeking to embody the highest moral standards, but also recognizing that in the world as we know it we sometimes have to choose lesser evils.
- **Stability and change** – preserving core values, but being flexible about everything else.
- **Sensitivity and resilience** – sensitivity on behalf of others, and resilience on one's own behalf, both of which are so important in nursing an organization through a process of controversial change.

I have gone through this list not just by way of reminder of what has been covered during the previous chapters. It is actually crucial to the role of leaders that they are striking balances, and having to strike good balances, all the time. As if all this was not enough, there is also the balance to be struck between the area of life in which they exercise leadership, and the rest of their lives. There is the balance to be found between work, spouse, children, the local community, church and other activities. What does it profit someone to be a successful leader, if they then become a stranger in their own homes, with an unhappy partner and neglected children? I have been very impressed by certain managing directors I know, who make it a matter of principle whenever possible, to be home in time to read the kids a story or tuck them up in bed.

Being a successful leader, then, is partly about the search for a balanced lifestyle. I do not underestimate the challenge of this in the present social and economic climate. It is hugely difficult. There are bound to be tensions involved. A friend who loves sailing has a lovely image of how tension can be creative: a well-trimmed yacht, careering along under the impact of creative tension between the wind and the sea, all combining to produce forward movement. It is a picture of poise under pressure. I suspect that the leaders whom we admire most manage to embody this.

These three definitions of success are complementary: attaining goals, developing potential, and performing a balancing act. What each of them has in common is the idea of doing something well. When something is done well, it is right and proper to take pleasure in it. The British tend to be suspicious of successful people – and so do many Christians – but there is no intrinsic reason why success is not acceptable to God. We must beware of a kind of Christian masochism, of seeking comfort too easily in failure, which can serve as an excuse for all kinds of incompetence and mediocrity. Despite branding Jesus as history's greatest failure, Maria Boulding is also at pains to note that 'there was no cult of failure in Jesus' life and there should be none in ours. He rejoiced in his strength and intelligence and used them to the full; he did his utmost to succeed. So should we.'[9]

Asking Questions about Success

Success, however, has its dangers. It can easily lure us into a state of complacency. We must not allow ourselves to be carried away or corrupted by success. If God means us to succeed, he certainly does not wish us to *succumb* to success. The Old Testament story of King Solomon can help us here. It tells us about a man who began by putting God first in his life. He was rewarded with the gift of wisdom, initiated impressive building projects, forged valuable tactical alliances, and came to acquire all the trappings of success. But somewhere along the line, Solomon went sadly astray. His wealth, fame and an excess of foreign wives had a corrupting effect on him. One verse from the story puts its finger on the problem: 'his heart was not wholly true to the Lord his God' (1 Kings 11.4).

The book of Jeremiah contains some advice which Solomon could usefully have heeded, and which any present-day success-story might also benefit from considering. It says:

'Let not the wise man boast of his wisdom
or the strong man boast of his strength
or the rich man boast of his riches,
but let him who boasts boast about this:
that he understands and knows me,
that I am the Lord, who exercises kindness,
justice and righteousness on earth,
for in these I delight,' declares the Lord.
Jeremiah 9:23-4

The simple truth contained here is that nothing in life matters as much as knowing and understanding God.

What also helps to keep us humble is the recognition

that in this life, success is rarely unambiguous or unquali-
fied. £1000 million profit for ICI sounds wonderful, but
figures like that only make sense in the context of sales
and turnover. It is also reasonable to ask whether from the
biblical perspective of justice and righteousness, there may
not be such a thing as excessive profit: a level of profit
which indicates that some of the groups to whom a company owes responsibility are being harshly treated or even
cheated. In looking back and contemplating a successful
task, there is nearly always a sense of something that could
have been done better or have gone better.

On the issue of developing people's potential, one of the
leaders I know who does this best is the chairman of a
highly successful engineering firm in Yorkshire. His company evokes a strong sense of purposeful community, of
individuals having the space to blossom, and teams pulling
together in a cohesive way. All the more interesting, then,
that when I asked the chairman whether he had experienced any failures, he felt these consisted largely in people
who had not developed as much as they might, such as the
senior welder whose promotion had not worked out. The
higher the standards one sets oneself, the more one is dis-
appointed by anything that falls short of them.

Let us return to the matter of balance. The fact is that
it seems impossible to be perfectly balanced all the time.
There are periods when a company's objectives have to be
sharply prioritized. Sometimes this means an all-out struggle for survival. Or think of the way we relate to people:
sometimes it is important that others see the big heart in
us, at other times we may need to present the inner steel.
There are times when work is all-consuming, and it is necessary to work flat out for a limited period and then give
ourselves a breather. Our yacht is constantly being blown
off course by the force of wind, tide or other circumstances.
And when we measure success in terms of development
and growth, we have to admit that this does not occur

according to a steady linear progression. We experience some pretty sharp oscillations. We feel buffeted from pillar to post.

However, it is still worth asking: can we become more competent in dealing with these crises? Can we behave more calmly through the process of oscillation? Can we acquire a greater objectivity, so that we are able to make sound judgements when the pressure is really on? I believe that the quality of our relationship with God is the key to all these things. We need to find, or preserve, a still centre in the midst of our busy lives, a point where we make time to be still and at peace with our God. There is an old but true saying that if you are too busy to have time to pray, you are too busy. Maintaining a consistent prayer rhythm in our lives - a rhythm that varies from person to person - is crucial to discovering a better balance and greater peace of mind.[10]

Plumbing the Depths of Failure

As we all know, success is not the whole story. The fact is that in the workplace everyone, sooner or later, experiences failure - failure not just of a partial or trivial kind, but serious failure. Targets go unmet, a new product flops, relationships break down, customers express their dissatisfaction, the media gives our organization a hard time. The company may even go bankrupt. The list of horrible things that can happen is endless.

Failure in our place of work can be absolutely miserable and personally demoralizing. Recognition of this is what is missing in the writing of Tom Peters. For all his peculiar way of putting things, Peters is actually on to an important point: that failures which are well thought out, speedily executed, quickly adjusted, and thoroughly learned from, should be supported by management. But he does not take sufficiently seriously the pain which failure brings. Stephen

Pattison, author of a helpful chapter on failure in his book
A Critique of Pastoral Care, describes it in this way: 'Failure
brings in its wake that most terrible of feelings, shame, a
sense of complete exposure and vulnerability.'[11] It is the
feeling of having let ourselves and other people down. It is
the feeling of wanting the earth to open beneath our feet
and swallow us up, to remove us from the eyes of scorn,
the mouths of ridicule and the fingers of blame.

Pattison, writing about the subject of pastoral care,
makes the interesting point that failure is particularly difficult to endure for the person who consciously devotes
himself to helping others. There is failure in pastoral care as
in every other area of life; some carers do more harm than
good. Failure in altruism is an especially cruel experience.

The pain of failure is also very acute for leaders. Leaders
cannot isolate their own performance and reputation from
that of the people they lead. They are often the scapegoats,
carrying the can, feeling personally implicated in the failure
of their enterprise. We are fooling ourselves if we try to
pretend that this is not profoundly painful.

In the previous chapter, I described the story of a charity in which the process of managing change badly misfired.
It provoked strong resentment among staff who felt they
had not been consulted. The director of the charity then
heroically submitted himself to an exhausting schedule of
going round the country, listening to how staff felt about
what had happened. Again and again he heard the cry:
'Why have you done this to us?' After thirty-five such
meetings in forty working days, he was shattered. He had
soaked up wave after wave of anger, and was near to
breaking point.

As the director of the charity described this experience
to me, I could not help thinking of what Jesus went
through on the cross.[12] Clearly, there are many aspects of
the crucifixion which take it beyond the sphere of normal
human suffering. It is one excrutiating form of physical

punishment that is no longer practised; and the element of taking the weight of humanity's sin upon himself, of being 'wounded for our transgressions', was unique to Jesus. But all who have found themselves the target of spiteful, scape-goating human behaviour can identify with elements in the passion story.

Jesus was mocked and derided by passers-by, the Roman soldiers, the chief priests, and at least one of the criminals who was crucified with him. He soaked up wave after wave of hostility. Some of the insults were probably hurled by people who knew little about him; there are always folk ready to join in a popular act of condemning someone, from a position of partial ignorance. Others may well have been people who a week before had cheered him on his entry into Jerusalem. Jesus experienced the full force of human fickleness. Many leaders who are the targets of criticism know just how transitory friendship and support can be. A leader under fire, one who is considered to have failed, can suddenly become a very lonely person.

Failing Forward

And yet the fact is that failure need not be totally negative. It can be a great learning experience. Often we learn more from the experience of failure than we do from the experience of success. The reason is not hard to find. We take success more easily for granted. We do not stop and analyse the reasons why we have been successful. Failure makes us stop and work out where we went wrong. We identify things we resolve to avoid in future. I have heard of an investment manager in California who makes it his habit to invest in people who have failed rather than in those who have been successful. His reasoning is that pride comes before a fall, and those who have failed are likely to be more worldly-wise next time round.

But it cannot be assumed that this learning process will

be automatic. Some people do make the same mistakes again and again. Others respond to a failure in one direction by over-compensating, and making an equally serious blunder in the opposite direction. Those who play golf will know the mortification of leaving a five-foot putt six inches short of the hole. You resolve to hit the ball harder next time. An hour later, you are faced with a similar length putt, and what happens? You knock the ball three feet past. You failed to take into account the fact that in the meantime the sun had dried the greens out, and this time you were putting on a slight downhill slope. There are plenty of working equivalents to this experience. When we think we are in a similar situation to one in which we experienced failure previously, it is important to take account of factors about the new situation which may be subtly different. Learning from failure is a complex and far from straightforward process.

I want to suggest some very basic steps that will help us to learn from failure, and to discover the art of what I call *failing forward*. These three steps are: accurate assessment, admitting and apologizing, and appropriate amendment.

1. Accurate Assessment

First of all, we need to assess the nature and extent of the failure accurately. Like success, failure is a relative concept. Consider an example from another field of sporting endeavour, that of snooker. Jimmy White is widely regarded as a failure because he has lost the world championship snooker final six times. But his consistency in reaching the final still makes him a very successful player – more so in fact than nearly everyone but the player he keeps losing to, Stephen Hendry.

Failure can also be very subjective. Stephen Pattison comments that 'people's own evaluation of their success or

failure may be wildly at odds with the evaluation of others;
hence the phenomenon of people condemning themselves
as failures while being celebrated by others for the very
thing they think they have failed at.'[13] The converse may
also be true: that we delude ourselves that we have been
successful, when there are actually lots of hurt and angry
people muttering about us behind our backs. In order to
come to a more objective assessment, it is important to
encourage people to be open, and to glean feedback from
a wide range of people who are affected by our actions.
Even then, however, the disparity contained within the
feedback may leave us puzzled and frustrated.

I run a course in a federation of theological colleges,
where there is a considerable span of theological view
and educational attainment. After several years of reading
students' evaluation sheets, I have reached the conclusion
that it is impossible to please everybody. In this and in
other areas of life, we need to take the critical and negative
comments seriously, without losing sight of the affirming
and positive ones, and try to arrive at some balanced
judgement.

As an aid to accurate assessment, it is often helpful to
consult an individual, or perhaps a group, whose judgement
we have learnt to trust, to ask for their candid opinion.
Ideally they will be people who have a good understanding
of the situation under review, but are not too closely
involved. In other words, they are a well-informed, but
external, reference-point. They should be people we can
consider as friends, but not sycophantic yes-men who are
unwilling to voice unpopular truths. When King David
experienced his most notorious moral failure – committing
adultery with Bathsheba and engineering the death of her
husband – he only acknowledged the gravity of his offence
after being confronted with a telling parable by the
prophet Nathan (2 Samuel 12.1–15). Nathan clearly saw

an evil to which David, in his infatuation, had become blinded.

In the commercial context, accurate assessment is complicated by the tension between short-term and long-term perspectives. Superficially successful results can sometimes be the product of creative accounting, a polished veneer concealing the grim reality of downward trends and a dispirited workforce. Superficially poor results can sometimes be a one-off, a temporary blip interrupting a steady period of growth. What looks like failure in the short-term may actually constitute far-sighted investment, the necessary cost which is the prelude to future success.

Leaders are often under enormous pressure to deliver positive results in the short term, to bolster morale and reassure financial investors. But leaders who have integrity will not be overwhelmed by such pressure. There are moments when it is vitally important that leaders hold their nerve, and encourage people to be patient. In the capacity of overseer, which we looked at in chapter four, leaders may actually be able to see the overall situation better than anyone else. They are in the best position to make an accurate assessment. They may need to educate people, both inside and outside the organization, about the true state of affairs. This might mean a company chairman spending time with the investment analysts!

Another situation is where an individual or group pursue a particular option, such as research and development on a new product, which turns out, after considerable expenditure of time, money and energy, to be a dead end. This is a particularly common phenomenon in the pharmaceuticals industry. For every drug which gets through all the trial stages, and reduces the sum of human suffering, there are many which fall by the wayside. It is very hard for a group of research scientists to admit after several years that clinical trials are not producing the results they had hoped for, or that the drug they developed is what people in the industry call a 'me too' – a drug which is a mere imitation of one produced by a rival firm, and has no distinctive qualities which can be honestly marketed. Objectivity tends to be a quality in short supply in such circumstances. The scientific data may indicate that the late cancellation of a drug of dubious merit is the right and proper thing to do, but the internal and external pressures to carry on are enormous.

All the more praiseworthy, then, is the leader who acts with courage and integrity in that situation. When an option has been thoroughly researched, and the results are negative or unconvincing, ceasing to pursue that option should not be dubbed a failure. It is more a case of *withdrawing with honour*. But inevitably, not everyone will see it that way. People are hungry for quick successes, not time-consuming failures. Clearly, the quicker that failure can be recognized, and the failed course of action abandoned, the better (these are the sort of failures Tom Peters looks for and celebrates). But the fact is that some avenues of research do demand very thorough inquiry before you know which way you should go.

2. Admitting and Apologising

Let us now assume that an accurate assessment of a course of action or overall performance within an organization has been carried out, and the verdict is, to a significant degree, negative. In other words, failure is not just a malicious rumour; it amounts to objective reality. Things have gone seriously wrong. The second important step is to *admit it*. This sounds so obvious that it is scarcely worth saying, but many people will go to enormous lengths to avoid admitting failure.

A senior manager in one of Britain's major clearing banks encountered this problem when the bank introduced their first credit card. The mechanics of the process had not been sufficiently thought through; the computer systems they had in operation were inadequate for the complexity of the task; enormous resources had to be poured in to keep the credit card going. It was a loss-maker for a full six years. But because so much prestige had been invested in the card, the corporate culture found it impossible to admit to failure. The consequence was that lessons were learnt, and mistakes were put right, much more slowly than would otherwise have been the case. We have to acknowledge failure before we can resume forward momentum.

Christians should be well-practised at admitting failure. In many church traditions, Christians confess their sins every week and receive, through the words of a minister, the assurance of pardon and forgiveness. At the heart of the Christian gospel is the message of forgiveness, the possibility of putting the past behind us and starting anew. These are not just 'nice' sentiments which are relevant only to what we do at home and school, at church and in the local community – though forgiveness is needed, often desperately needed, in all those situations. Confession and forgiveness are profound realities which impinge upon the tough world of organizational and commercial life. There, too, admitting failure can be enormously liberating; it can do wonders for the healing of wounded human relationships.

Research into customer perception has shown that when an organization admits to making mistakes, and acts promptly to remedy them, the people who are affected think more of the organization rather than less. The converse is also true. When I gave the second of the London lectures, I had a bad experience on my train journeys both to and from London. Each journey was badly delayed. What really annoyed me was not the inadequacies of the service – the signal failure at Hackney Down, or whatever – but the complete failure to apologize for the inconvenience caused. No admission of failure; a significant decline in customer confidence – there is a notable correlation between the two.

There are times, of course, when admitting error means confessing on other people's behalf. This is something which often falls on the person at the top of an organization, but it happens to people lower down the line as well. Think for a moment about a technical service engineer, who in the course of carrying out routine maintenance work receives a mouthful from a customer complaining of faulty goods or a late delivery. He could easily say, with a jerk of the thumb, 'it wasn't me, it was them back at the works', because others in his company are responsible for the mistakes which have been made. But it is actually much more constructive, and he is much more likely to reconcile the customer, if he finds the grace to say 'I'm sorry' on behalf of the organization. In a sense, an engineer who does that redeems the situation by taking the blame vicariously. There is something quasi-redemptive about his action, though he probably doesn't realize it!

There are problems about publicly admitting failure. Some failures within organizations are internal matters, the effects can be contained from the public. The bank which failed with its credit card largely succeeded in doing that. If the general public are not aware of any problems, it seems unnecessary to let them know about them. In some situations, there is an understandable legal concern that admitting failure leaves one open to the danger of being sued and taken to court. Clearly, the quality of astuteness is called for in these matters. In many situations, however, the danger of legal action is minimal. An apology is all that people are looking for. An apology is what restores credibility.

3. Appropriate Amendment

In other cases, however, an apology by itself is clearly not enough. Actions as well as words are required. This brings us to the third step in our response to failure, which is to amend our course of action. Sometimes amendment may take the form of atonement, of reparation for the damage which has been done to people: the reimbursed fare for the customer whose train delay meant he never arrived at a crucial meeting; the generous compensation for the employee who was wrongfully dismissed. In other cases it will be prompt action which does not constitute an admission of legal liability, but shows a proper regard for public safety: the retailer removing from the shelves products which have been linked with an outbreak of food poisoning; the airline grounding and checking its planes in the wake of an unexplained crash.

Something also needs to be said about amendment in terms of exercising discipline within an organization. Consider again the case of the unfortunate service engineer, apologizing on behalf of his colleagues. The fact is that taking responsibility for the mistakes of others is not something anyone should have to put up with indefinitely. How forgiving can a leader afford to be of subordinates' mistakes? This is a complex question which resists an easy answer. There are three major types of mistake. There is the mistake which is not in the least culpable, but is actually the result of an innovative spirit: the new process, product or tactic which was worth trying, but doesn't actually work. These are the sort of failures which Peters says deserve praise, not blame, as long as lessons are learnt from them swiftly. Then there are mistakes which result from carelessness, sloppiness or downright incompetence: a leader should be much less tolerant of these, but give people the opportunity to show they can do better. Finally there are mistakes of a moral nature, where employees are dishonest, manipulative or do something which plainly contravenes the company's ethical code. A good leader is least tolerant of this type of failing.

We see here another balance of qualities emerging, that of being both firm and forgiving. I know a company doctor who is convinced that in order to manage a business out of decline, a ritual bloodletting is required. 'There must be blood on the floor', are his memorable words. By this he means, typically, giving some miscreant a good rollicking, in a loud voice and a public place, so that everyone knows there has been a good rollicking. It may well be that there is a place for public expressions of righteous indignation in exceptional circumstances, but the danger here is that people may be scapegoated unfairly, with a consequent loss of morale in the organization. I suggest that a Christian leadership approach is one that leaves no room for doubt that radical improvement is needed, but shows a solidarity with the failures of the group and a readiness to forgive individual mistakes. This should create a climate in which people are far readier to acknowledge and learn from what they have done wrong.

Finally, there is amendment where the experience of failure leads one to alter a corporate course of strategy, or to explore a different niche of the market. Failure to sell a product prompts one to ask a whole variety of questions. Is there a market for the product? Do we have the right people to sell the product? Are we in touch with people who might want it? Has the product been packaged in the wrong way? Does the product need to be subtly different? Is a whole different kind of product called for? The answers to such questions can set in motion a significantly altered strategy for the organization.

Lady Judith Wilcox, who chaired one of my London lectures, has 'confessed' to an episode in her business career when she made a serious mistake – but one which proved very instructive. Near the start of her career, she was running a family business of high-street shops in the south-west of England. Trading in shellfish gave her the idea of buying two fishing trawlers as a sideline. But owning and running a trawler proved very different from running shops. The price of oil soared, the costs of running the boats escalated, and Cornish women began to lose enthusiasm for going down to the quay to buy unfilleted fish. The business sank to the point where its owner suffered the shame of watching a writ being nailed to one ship, and the other being registered as a wreck.

This was a humiliating experience, but it had a constructive effect in terms of focusing the mind. Judith realized what she was really good at: organizing people and buildings on dry land. She also learnt lessons about the way the fishing industry was going. Seeing that the future lay with those who added value to the basic product of fish, by making it easier to cook and tastier to eat, she moved into the processing industry. She set up Channel Foods, a company which specialized in smoked fish, and which eventually became very successful. Failure led Judith to alter her line of business, and the end result was highly productive.

Failure therefore calls for three important responses: accurate assessment; admission and apology; and amendment which results in an appropriate course of action. If we do learn practical lessons from episodes of failure, we can actually *fail forward*: the one step back can actually be followed by two steps forward. Leaders have the responsibility not only of learning from their mistakes, but of helping others to do so.

However, it should not be pretended that reversing the effects of failure is easy. There is no doubt that once the sniff of failure has been let loose, it grows very quickly into a stench. People love to gossip about things that go wrong. Even where the process outlined above is carried out, it may take time for confidence to be restored, both inside and outside the organization.

An interesting example of this is the Church Commissioners, who in the space of a couple of years in the early 1990s became something of a laughing-stock as far as the Church of England was concerned. What actually happened was that during the 1980s the Commissioners took on more financial responsibilities in the church than they could really sustain. A key event here was the commitment made back in 1983 to guarantee clergy for the first time a decent pension. In the late 1980s the Commissioners also borrowed money to indulge in some dubious property speculation. This went badly wrong. In the face of the ensuing recession, the properties built could not be let, and some assets had to be sold off to pay back the borrowings. The result was that the Commissioners' property assets declined in value from just under £3 billion in 1989, to £2.2 billion in 1992. The headline 'Church loses £800 million' has featured in a big way in the secular press, and the loss has been blamed for the fact that dioceses are now being expected to find a lot more of the money to pay clergy stipends. Not surprisingly, morale in the pew and motivation to give sank to a low ebb.

Clearly the Church Commissioners did make serious errors of judgment. (I also have questions to ask about their practice from an ethical point of view, and have indeed served on a working party which argued for a more coherent ethical approach to their investment policy.)[14] However, the figures which have made such a splash in the media need to be put into context. For some twenty years prior to the late 1980s, the Commissioners had an extremely successful record of investment. Nobody gives them much credit for that. Moreover, property values oscillate up and down all the time. If you take as points of comparison two different years – 1985, when the portfolio was valued at £1.9 billion, and 1994, when it was running at about £2.5 billion – the picture looks rather better.

The Commissioners also acted reasonably promptly to

put things right. They have been honest about the extent of the problem and the mistakes they made. They commissioned a proper report undertaken by the accountants Coopers & Lybrand into what happened,[15] they have made changes in personnel and adjusted their policies in the light of the report's criticisms, and they have also apologized to General Synod. So they cannot be accused of complacency or cover-up. The failure was not actually of such gargantuan proportions and long-lasting implications that the decline in congregational morale is justified. In the long run, it probably makes sense for the Commissioners to concentrate mainly on providing for clergy pensions, and the congregations to take major responsibility for paying stipends – a shift which is being accelerated by this recent failure.[16]

In terms of my three steps – assessment, admission and amendment – the Church Commissioners appear to have followed them all. Where I think they were at fault in the process of responding to failure was in not seeking to communicate the true facts of the situation at a popular level, to the person in the pew. It is no good expecting the ordinary person to read largely inaccessible reports. Communication at the level of the *Daily Mail* as well as the *Financial Times* is what is required. It underlines the importance of the quality of good communication – a priceless asset in the restoration of confidence and recovery from failure.

Taking Neither Success Nor Failure Too Seriously

An underlying conviction of this book is that how Christians behave in the secular world is crucially important. If we take seriously Jesus' assertion that his followers are the salt of the earth and the light of the world, the consequence is that we care deeply, and should be seen to care deeply, about what goes on in the workplace. If our role is one of leader, the extent and quality of that care should be all the greater. Nevertheless, I would like to suggest that in the final reckoning, the Christian faith helps us to take neither success nor failure too seriously. It ought ideally to give us a certain *detachment*, without taking anything away in terms of *commitment*.

The issue at stake here is where we find our core identity. One very common aspect of failing is that it can for a time consume our whole identity. We do not say 'I have failed', or 'I failed in this respect', but all too often we say the bleak words of self-condemnation: 'I am a failure'. Failure is felt as a total experience of one's whole being. As such, it is almost certainly not an accurate verdict. We may have failed in some things; we have probably succeeded in others. But we feel a failure – full stop.

Yet as Christians, the value we place upon ourselves should not depend on what we do or don't achieve, whether at work or anywhere else. We need to remember that God alone is the ultimate judge of the success we have made of our lives. His verdict may turn out to be very different, both from our own verdict and other people's. In any case, the predominant mode in which he relates to us is not that of judge. He relates to us first and foremost as our saviour, and because of this, he is also our ultimate security.

When we plumb the depths of failure, we can therefore be sustained by the love of God, which is not conditional on whether we have landed a crucial contract, or saved a company from disaster. To encourage us through the dark and difficult times we need to be thoroughly 'soaked in grace', a lovely phrase which is a favourite of Hugo de Waal, the Bishop of Thetford. It is God who can save us from being carried away by our successes; he can also save us from being devastated by our failures. It is because our core identity consists in being a child of God, loved by God, sustained by God and redeemed by God, that it is possible to have a certain detachment about the issues we grapple with from Monday to Friday.

The apostle Paul writes these heart-warming words:

> We know that in everything God works for good for those who love him, who are called according to his purpose . . . If God is for us, who is against us? . . . It is God who justifies; who is to condemn? . . . Who shall separate us from the love of Christ? Shall tribulation, or distress, or persecution, or famine, or nakedness, or peril, or sword? . . . No, in all these things we are more than conquerors through him who loved us. For I am sure that neither death, nor life, nor angels, nor principalities, nor things present, nor things to come, nor powers, nor height, nor depth, nor anything else in all creation, will be able to separate us from the love of God in Christ Jesus our Lord.
> *Romans 8.31–9*

Here is a little exercise to do on completion of this book. Read those last two verses, Romans 8.38–9, and substitute for 'death', 'life', 'angels', and the other key words, all the things that matter to you in your working life. Include the positive things as well as the negative, the successes as well as the failures, the contracts you won as well as the contracts you lost, the relationships which worked well and the relationships which turned sour, the best-selling product and the one which ended up in the reject bin. You will not be doing violence to the sense of scripture! Paul actually says 'anything else in all creation'. So throw them all in. Then pray over those verses until you really mean them and believe them.

It is by grounding ourselves afresh in the love of Christ, by acquiring the detachment to go alongside our commitment, by discovering again where our true roots lie, that we can return to the world inspired to change failure into success, to lead people on to something better, to practise anew the elusive art of failing forward. Hidden in the ashes of many a wretched failure lie the seeds of many an exciting transformation.

Suffering

See what a transformation!
Those hands so active and powerful
Now are tied, alone and fainting,
You see where your work ends.
But you are confident still, and gladly commit
What is rightful into a stronger hand,
And say that you are contented.
You were free for a moment of bliss,
Then you yielded your freedom
Into the hand of God
That he might perfect it in glory.
Dietrich Bonhoeffer[17]

6

Satraps and Exiles

Seeking the Welfare of the City

Is it worth it? If readers are not already aware of this from
their personal experience, the observations and reflections
offered in the previous pages make it clear that the exercise
of leadership is often fraught with struggle and difficulty.
Being a leader involves a heavy discharge of responsibility.
Becoming a leader usually requires a major investment of
time and energy. But at the end of the day, is it all 'vanity
and a striving after wind' (Ecclesiastes 2.26)?

There are certainly plenty of warnings in scripture against
putting too many of our hopes and aspirations in earthly,
as opposed to heavenly, realities. Hebrews 11 speaks of the
men and women of faith, whose forward-looking mentality
showed that 'they were strangers and exiles on the earth'.
What they desired was 'a better country, that is, a heavenly one. Therefore God is not ashamed to be called their
God, for he has prepared for them a city' (Hebrews 11.16).

The question I asked in chapter one – why bother? –
therefore needs to be faced again. If we are strangers and
exiles on the earth, if – as an old hymn says – 'This earth
is not my home, I'm just a-passing through', is the massive
investment of energy which is needed to be a leader in a
secular world justified? Are we not all too likely to be lured
away by the preoccupations and pressures which threaten
to lead us into worshipping false lords and into serving
worldly masters who are quite different from the God and
Father of our Lord Jesus Christ?

The danger of such apostasy is very real. Some people

commit it. Others hover on the edge of doing so. And yet I believe the temptation of withdrawing into an other-worldly pietism should be firmly resisted. We must take seriously our status as exiles, but still involve ourselves fully in the world. For some people this may entail taking on the mantle of leadership.

It is very instructive to consider the letter which the prophet Jeremiah sent to the people of Jerusalem, who had been taken into exile in Babylon by King Nebuchadnezzar. It said:

> Thus says the Lord of hosts, the God of Israel, to all the exiles whom I have sent into exile from Jerusalem to Babylon: Build houses and live in them; plant gardens and eat their produce. Take wives and have sons and daughters; take wives for your sons, and give your daughters in marriage, that they may bear sons and daughters; multiply there, and do not decrease. But seek the welfare of the city where I have sent you into exile, and pray to the Lord on its behalf, for in its welfare you will find your welfare . . .
> *Jeremiah* 29. 4–7

This is remarkable advice. Later on in his book, Jeremiah pronounces oracles of doom and judgement on Babylon for all its arrogance and inquiry. He was under no illusions about its failings. But here he takes a different tack. Contrary to those who were predicting a short exile, Jeremiah forecasts a sizeable stay of at least two generations. He advises the Jews to accept their exile and to settle down to a normal existence in Babylon: building houses, planting gardens, getting married – all the stuff of everyday life. But the attitude he advocates towards Babylon goes well beyond passive toleration. 'Seek the welfare of the city,' he says, 'and pray to the Lord on its behalf, for in its welfare you will find your welfare.' This suggests active concern and active involvement.

What happens in our secular, or even pagan, environment should not be considered a matter of irrelevance or indifference. It affects us in all sorts of ways, for good and evil, and we should be doing our utmost to shape it by our actions and our prayers. If the analogy between Jeremiah's description of the appropriate Jewish response to a situation of exile and Christians' current situation of 'being in the world but not of the world' holds good, there is a clear biblical rationale for involvement of the type I have been describing in this book.

I like to think that one of the exiles who heard or read Jeremiah's letter was the young man Daniel. Indeed, I find it difficult to understand the audacity of Daniel's career without the sense of his having a mandate from a great man of God. For Daniel and his friends, seeking the welfare of Babylon meant being prepared to serve in Nebuchadnezzer's government. Remarkably, Daniel outlived the Babylon empire, and even saw its overthrow and replacement by the Medo-Persian empire. Daniel must have been a very old man by the time he had his narrow shave in the lions' den under King Darius. Through much of that time he occupied ministerial office, holding his own among a world of satraps, sages and sorcerers, who often sought to outwit and oust him.

It is important to note that in order to be able to serve, Daniel and his friends were prepared to accommodate themselves to the Babylonian court to a considerable degree. In Daniel chapter one, we read that they were educated for three years, learning 'the language and literature of the Babylonians' (Daniel 1.4–5). This involved immersion in a completely alien thought-world, characterized by astrology, polytheism, and spiritual dualism. Yet it was only by absorbing themselves in this foreign culture that they could be equipped to serve God in it. They passed whatever educational tests there were with flying colours: 'as for these four youths, God gave them learning and skill in all letters and wisdom' (Daniel 1.17).

In a similar way, most Christians who aspire to leadership in today's world have to acquaint themselves thoroughly with current thinking in their chosen area, and prove their competence by passing examinations and showing their mettle. This can often feel like a long and arduous haul. Some of what is received at the hands of their teachers will indeed be inimical to their understanding of God, Christian doctrine and Christian ethics. Daniel, Shadrach, Meshach and Abednego must have been very firmly rooted in the faith of their forefathers in order to pass through this Babylonian training school, with their trust in God sure and their morality uncorrupted.

Even during this apprentice stage, Daniel and his friends showed that they were prepared to be different. Interestingly, they accepted the change of names given to them by the chief eunuch (Daniel 1.7). Some of these name-changes incorporated references to the deities of Babylon, and could therefore be regarded as suspect. However, it was not on this issue that they chose to make an objection, but on the question of food. Daniel believed it was important to stick by the Israelite food laws. In a sense the question of which issue he took a stand on is not the important matter; rather the fact that he did take a stand, and at an early stage, so that he showed his ultimate loyalty was to his God, and not the king. But he would never have got away with this had he not received a sympathetic hearing from the chief of eunuchs. Without doubting that God 'gave Daniel favour and compassion in his sight' (Daniel 1.10), it is plausible to suppose that Daniel had an attractive, winsome personality which held him and his friends in good stead.

By taking a courageous stand and experiencing God's faithfulness at this point, Daniel, Shadrach, Meshach and

Abednego prepared the way for the sterner tests which came later: the fiery furnace and the lions' den. They showed that their willingness to participate constructively in the governing structures of Babylon was not willingness at any cost. They put down a marker. For those who long to lead with integrity, to bring a spirit of moral reform to an organization, there is a significant lesson here. There will need to be some measure of accommodation to the prevailing culture of the organization as one progresses through the ranks, but from the very outset, a readiness to draw lines and say 'no' should be apparent. It would be a contradiction of the very idea of integrity if one were to discover a sudden enthusiasm for the concept only when one reaches the dizzy heights of power. In any case, an appetite for integrity will probably have long disappeared if it has lain dormant for twenty years or so. Daniel's reputation was so secure that even when his enemies did their best to discover a skeleton in his cupboard – some sloppy piece of administration? an allegation of corruption? – 'they could find no ground for complaint or any fault, because he was faithful, and no error or fault was found in him' (Daniel 6.4).

It would be intriguing to know more of how Daniel went about the daily routine of public service. What changes did he initiate? What reforms did he introduce? To what extent was he able to temper the grandiose designs of Nebuchadnezzar? We are given details of what he did only at the moments of crisis, when kings were troubled by dreams and his own life was under threat. But those moments are very revealing, and from them we can draw three important concluding lessons about transforming leadership.

First, Daniel genuinely sought the welfare of others. When King Nebuchadnezzar became furious – rather unreasonably – that his wise men could not interpret a dream which he could not even remember, he gave orders that they should be destroyed. Daniel showed concern not only for his own skin but for that of the wise men in securing a stay of execution. 'Why is the decree of the king so severe?' he asked (Daniel 2.15). 'Do not destroy the wise men of Babylon; bring me in before the king, and I will show the king the interpretation' (Daniel 2.24). When his success in this matter led to a spectacular promotion, Daniel secured strategic appointments for his three friends as well (Daniel 2.49).

In chapter four, when Daniel found himself asked to interpret another of Nebuchadnezzar's dreams, he was moved to great dismay when he realized the unhappy fate in store for the king. It is quite possible that Daniel had developed a genuine affection for the erratic despot whom he served. But this did not prevent him from challenging Nebuchadnezzar to change his style of government, and demonstrate justice and mercy, in the hope that God's judgement on the king might be allayed (Daniel 4.27). Daniel was a man of sensitive feeling, anxious to avoid distress for those below, alongside and above him. In a similar way, Christians at work will rightly feel bonds of affection and concern for those who do not share their faith.

Second, Daniel was rooted in a regular life of prayer. Jeremiah exhorted the exiles to pray, and Daniel took him at his word. His practice was public knowledge. In his house he had windows in his upper chamber open towards Jerusalem, 'and he got down on his knees three times a day and gave thanks before his God' (Daniel 6.10). When he knew that the satraps were scheming against him, and that his habit of prayer threatened his very life, he continued to do exactly the same thing. Daniel was doubtless a busy man, but he was not too busy to pray. He made 'petition and supplication before his God', and he did not mind people knowing it. His regular prayer life sustained him through the difficult assignment of serving God in a strange land. It was also a demonstration that his ultimate loyalty was not to any earthly master, Babylonian, Persian or otherwise.

Third, Daniel did not lose touch with his own people. The very fact that he prayed with his windows open towards Jerusalem is significant. Daniel still saw Jerusalem as his earthly home, and looked forward to the time predicted by Jeremiah, when God would restore the exiles to their own land (Jeremiah 29.10–14). He still identified passionately with his people, as is evident from the great prayer which is recorded in chapter nine. For all his nobility of character, he readily acknowledges that 'we have sinned', admitting the legitimacy of the judgement experienced by Judah and Israel. The prayer ends with a great invocation: 'O Lord, listen! O Lord, forgive! O Lord hear and act! For your sake, O my God, do not delay, because your city and your people bear your Name' (Daniel 9.19, NIV).

This prayer shows that through all his long record of public service, Daniel had kept in touch with his roots. Some Christians may shy away from heavy involvement in the secular world, because they fear that it means being less committed to their brothers and sisters in the church. It will indeed mean spending less time with them, but the example of Daniel suggests that it need not mean any lessening of concern for them and identification with them.

Not all of us are called to be leaders, and even fewer are pitched into situations which call for the heroism and extraordinary qualities of a Daniel. But his story, along with others in the Bible, makes clear that there is a place in God's purposes for people like him. God wants men and women who are prepared to apply their gifts and intelligence in the operations of a secular world, to immerse themselves in the world while remaining uncorrupted by it, and to exercise leadership in shaping this world for good. Strangers and exiles we may be, but God gives to most of us – like the Jewish exiles – some seventy years, in order to use profitably in his service. We all need to find our contemporary equivalent of Babylon, the earthly city whose welfare we should actively seek.

Notes

Chapter 1

1. John Finney, *Understanding Leadership* (Daybreak 1989).
2. Luther's teaching in this area is helpfully summarized both in Paul Althaus, *The Ethics of Martin Luther* (Fortress 1972), and Gustaf Wingren, *The Christian's Calling: Luther on Vocation* (Oliver & Boyd 1958).
3. Andrew Stokes, *Working with God: Faith and Life at Work* (Mowbray 1992), p. 44.
4. Christian Schumacher, *To Live and Work: A Theological Interpretation* (MARC Europe 1987).
5. See *To Live and Work*, chapter 10.
6. Miroslav Volf, *Work in the Spirit: Towards a Theology of Work* (Oxford University Press 1991), p. 100.
7. Michael Wilcock, *I Saw Heaven Opened: The Message of Revelation* (IVP 1975), p. 211.
8. Roger Evans and Peter Russell, *The Creative Manager* (Unwin Paperbacks 1990), p. 13.

Chapter 2

1. John Sculley, *Odyssey: Pepsi to Apple* (Collins 1987).
2. See Alvin Toffler, *The Third Wave* (Pan 1981). The 'first wave' is the pre-industrial, agricultural age.
3. For example, Peter Drucker, *The Practice of Management* (Harper & Row 1954), *Management: Tasks, Responsibilities, Practices* (Heinemann 1974), *The Frontiers of Management* (Heinemann 1986).
4. *The Frontiers of Management*, p. 173.

5. Sundridge Park handout, 'A Short Summary of Management Principles'.

6. See James McGregor Burns, *Leadership* (Harper & Row 1978); Warren Bennis, *The Unconscious Conspiracy* (Amacon Press 1976).

7. Quoted in David Clutterbuck and Stuart Crainer, *The Decline and Rise of British Industry* (Mercury Books 1988), p. 125.

8. Published in Peter Drucker, *Managing for the Future* (Butterworth-Heinemann 1992), p. 103.

9. Quoted in Carol Kennedy, *Guide to the Management Gurus* (Century Business 1993), pp. 2–3.

10. Warren Bennis and Burt Nanus, *Leaders: Strategies for Taking Charge* (Harper & Row 1985); Warren Bennis, *On Becoming a Leader* (Hutchinson 1989).

11. *Leaders*, p. 21.

12. The importance of Burns' work in leadership theory is widely acknowledged, yet his influence remains confined to the one book *Leadership*.

13. Robert H. Waterman Jr., *The Renewal Factor* (Bantam Press 1988), p. 75.

14. See the evidence cited in Paul S. Kirkbride (ed.), *Human Resource Management* (Routledge 1994), chapter 3, 'Leadership in the European Context: some Queries'.

15. Ricardo Semler, *Maverick!* (Century 1993).

16. I have always felt that Nehemiah 4.6, 'So we built the wall . . . for the people had a mind to work', speaks volumes about Nehemiah's motivational abilities.

17. Craig R. Hickman, *Mind of a Manager, Soul of a Leader* (John Wiley & Sons 1990).

18. For an accurate understanding of what each of Hickman's phrases mean, readers are advised to consult his book.

19. See Malcolm Goldsmith and Martin Wharton, *Knowing Me – Knowing You: Exploring Personality Type and Temperament* (SPCK 1993), for a helpful introduction to Myers-Briggs.

20. In a lecture for the Cambridge Theological Federation by Tom Wright, Dean of Lichfield, 3 May 1994.

21. See R. Meredith Belbin, *Management Teams: Why They Succeed or Fail* (Butterworth-Heinemann 1981), and *Team Roles at Work* (Butterworth-Heinemann 1993).

22. In the interview in *Director*, quoted above.
23. Here I have drawn on John Finney's helpful categorization in chapter 2 of *Understanding Leadership*.
24. James M. Kouzes and Barry Z. Posner, *Credibility* (Jossey-Bass Publishers 1993), p. 185.
25. Robert Greenleaf, *Servant Leadership: a Journey into the Nature of Legitimate Power and Greatness* (Paulist Press 1977).
26. *Servant Leadership*, p. 7.
27. Alastair Campbell, *Rediscovering Pastoral Care* (Darton, Longman & Todd 1986), p. 27.
28. See my comments about the wise use of the world's resources on p. 7.

Chapter 3

1. The wisdom literature in the Bible consists of Job, Psalms, Proverbs and Ecclesiastes.
2. *Credibility*, pp. 14–15.
3. See for example, Nick Davies, *The Unknown Maxwell* (Sidgwick & Jackson 1992); Roy Greenslade, *Maxwell's Fall* (Simon & Schuster 1992).
4. Written by Thomas Keneally, the book was originally published as *Schindler's Ark*, and now as *Schindler's List* (Sceptre 1994).
5. Robert Solomon, *Ethics and Excellence: Cooperation and Integrity in Business* (Oxford University Press 1992), p. 168.
6. *Rediscovering Pastoral Care*, p. 12.
7. Robert Jackall, *Moral Mazes: The World of Corporate Managers* (Oxford University Press 1988).
8. *Moral Mazes*, p. 109.
9. The John Lewis Partnership has a particularly positive approach to employees who wish to raise ethical concerns. On the subject of whistleblowing, see Marlene Winfield, *Minding Your Own Business: Self-Regulation and Whistleblowing in British Companies* (Social Audit 1990).
10. Interestingly, the bank's Christian Fellowship became involved in the in-house debate on Third World debt. They provided the vice-chairman with a valuable sounding-board.

11. John Macquarrie and James Childress, eds., *A New Dictionary of Christian Ethics* (SCM Press 1986), p. 65.

12. Namely, CARE and the Central European Foundation, Bratislava.

13. A parallel might be drawn here with Oscar Schindler's blatant use of bribes to save the lives of Jews threatened by imminent extermination in wartime Krakow. I would be among those who feel such action was justified in those exceptional, 'one-off' circumstances. A charity is faced by situations which recur regularly, and needs to think very carefully about making a policy of acceding to extortionate demands.

14. Re-published by the Institute of Management in November 1992.

15. ibid.

16. In fact, the Body Shop has recently come in for sharp criticism about whether it does conform to its professed standards on animal testing. Organizations which put themselves on a moral pedestal are liable to attract the closest scrutiny. Anita Roddick's *Body and Soul* (Ebury Press 1991) is a colourful mix of autobiography and statement of Body Shop philosophy.

17. I argue on p. 8 that the aim of wealth creation, properly understood, actually combines providing a service and making money; they are two sides of the same coin. Non-commercial organizations may claim that they are not concerned with making money, but they do of course have to observe financial disciplines. At the very least they want to avoid incurring debt.

18. The game is called *Apocalypse!*, and was devised by Richard Higginson and Geoff Moore. It is designed for use on business school and company training programmes.

19. *Credibility*, pp. 17–18.

20. Mention of sharp practice calls to mind the parable of Jesus in which the central character, variously described as the dishonest steward or the shrewd manager, exhibits precisely that. Faced with the sack, he curries favour with his master's clients by reducing their debts (Luke 16.1–9). However, the astuteness I am commending is not of this nature. I do not think Jesus wanted people to emulate the steward's dishonesty, but the urgency with which he acted in a time of crisis.

21. An example of an organization which takes the theme of mutuality very seriously is the Woolwich Building Society. An article in *The Times*, 27 August 1994, makes clear that their chairman Alan McLintock and chief executive Donald Kirkham believe strongly in looking to the mutual interests of different groups rather than simply maximizing profits.

Chapter 4

1. John Harvey-Jones, *Making It Happen: Reflections on Leadership* (Fontana/Collins 1988), p. 124.
2. Phil O'Donovan, 'Information Technology: Now and the Next Generation', in *The Global Opportunities and Social Implications of Hi-Tech: examples from Information Technology in Cambridge* (Cambridge Science Park symposium 1994), p. 13.
3. For an authoritative and (considering he was a Name on three of the worst-affected syndicates) remarkably dispassionate account of recent history at Lloyd's, see Adam Raphael, *Ultimate Risk: The Inside Story of the Lloyd's Catastrophe* (Bantam Press 1994).
4. A case where rapid change has taken place successfully is the Brazilian company Semco, referred to in chapter 2. See Ricardo Semler, *Maverick!* (Century 1993).
5. Quoted in David Clutterbuck and Stuart Crainer, *Makers of Management: Men and Women who Changed the Business World* (Guild Publishing 1990), p. 190.
6. *Making It Happen*, pp. 144-5.
7. Peter Thompson, *Sharing the Success: The Story of NFC* (Collins 1990), p. 122. Like Sculley's book, Peter Thompson is well worth reading for his mixture of fascinating personal story and instructive reflection upon corporate style and structure.
8. Rosabeth Moss Kanter, *The Change Masters: Corporate Entrepreneurs at Work* (Allen & Unwin 1984), chapter 9.
9. See *Understanding Leadership*, chapter 6.
10. *The Change Masters*, pp. 296-298.

11. A. E. Harvey, *Strenuous Commands: The Ethics of Jesus* (SCM 1990), p. 180.

12. What made Timothy's case distinctive was that he had a Jewish mother (his father being Greek), but the text implies that it was concern to give Timothy good standing in the eyes of the Jews who lived in the area which led Paul to circumcize him.

Chapter 5

1. Tom Peters, *Thriving on Chaos: Handbook for a Management Revolution* (Pan 1989), p. 259.

2. *Thriving on Chaos*, p. 258.

3. Maria Boulding, *Gateway to Hope* (Fount 1985), p. 17.

4. *Thriving on Chaos*, p. 71.

5. *Thriving on Chaos*, p. 9.

6. John Lovatt, 'Jesus in the Workplace: Towards a Better Theology of Work', MC, Vol. XXXIV, p. 14. MC (now *Modern Believing*) is the journal of the Modern Churchpeople's Union.

7. Charles Handy, *The Empty Raincoat* (Hutchinson 1994), p. 269. Handy says he heard the story from Bishop Richard Harries.

8. This is a key element in the Teambuilding Dispositions developed by Christian Schumacher in his Work Restructuring consultancy.

9. *Gateway to Hope*, p. 73.

10. For an excellent book on prayer whose title bears an interesting parallel to this book, see James Houston, *The Transforming Friendship: A Guide to Prayer* (Lion 1989).

11. Stephen Pattison, *A Critique of Pastoral Care* (SCM Press 1988), p. 145.

12. For an interesting treatment of the cross as an experience of failure, see Russ Parker, *Free to Fail* (Triangle 1992), chapter 5.

13. *A Critique of Pastoral Care*, p. 148.

14. A report published as *Our Best Interest: Guidelines for Ethical Investment*, by the Christian Ethical Investment Group.

15. Their report formed part of the overall *Lambeth Group Report*, which is available from the Church Commissioners and from Church House.
16. An interesting book on the Church's attitude to money, which makes some different proposals on how the Church Commissioners should employ their resources, is Adrian Mann, *No Small Change: Money, Christians and the Church* (The Canterbury Press, Norwich, 1992).
17. 'Suffering' is part of a longer poem, 'Stations on the Road to Freedom', written by Dietrich Bonhoeffer. It is published in his *Letters and Papers from Prison* (SCM Press 1971), p. 371.

Index

147

The Society for Promoting Christian Knowledge (SPCK)
has as its purpose three main tasks:

- **Communicating the Christian faith in its rich
  diversity**
- **Helping people to understand the Christian faith
  and to develop their personal faith**
- **Equipping Christians for mission and ministry**

SPCK Worldwide runs a substantial grant programme to
support Christian literature and communication projects
in over 100 countries. Special schemes also provide books
for those training for ministry in many parts of the world.
All gifts to SPCK are spent wholly on these grant
programmes, without deductions.

SPCK Bookshops support the life of the Christian
community by making available a full range of Christian
literature and other resources, and by providing support
to bookstalls and book agents throughout the UK. SPCK
Bookshops' mail order department meets the needs of
overseas customers and those unable to have access to
local bookshops.

SPCK Publishing produces Christian books and
resources, covering a wide range of inspirational,
pastoral, practical and academic subjects. Authors are
drawn from many different Christian traditions, and
publications aim to meet the needs of a wide variety of
readers in the UK and throughout the world.

The Society does not necessarily endorse the individual
views contained in its publications, but hopes they
stimulate readers to think about and further develop
their Christian faith.

For further information about the Society, please write to:
SPCK, Holy Trinity Church, Marylebone Road,
London NW1 4DU, United Kingdom.
Telephone: 0171 387 5282